New Business: Next Steps

The all-in-one guide to managing, marketing and growing your small business

ED GOODMAN and ANN HAWKINS

Harlow, England • London • New York • Boston • San Francisco • Toronto • Sydney • Auckland • Singapore • Hong Kong
Tokyo • Seoul • Taipei • New Delhi • Cape Town • São Paulo • Mexico City • Madrid • Amsterdam • Munich • Paris • Milan

PEARSON EDUCATION LIMITED
Edinburgh Gate
Harlow CM20 2JE
United Kingdom
Tel: +44 (0)1279 623623
Web: www.pearson.com/uk

First published 2015 (print and electronic)

© Pearson Education Limited 2015 (print and electronic)

The rights of Ed Goodman and Ann Hawkins to be identified as authors of this work have been asserted by them in accordance with the Copyright, Designs and Patents Act 1988.

Pearson Education is not responsible for the content of third-party internet sites.

ISBN: 978-1-292-01766-2 (print)
       978-1-292-01768-6 (PDF)
       978-1-292-01770-9 (ePub)
       978-1-292-01767-9 (eText)

British Library Cataloguing-in-Publication Data
A catalogue record for the print edition is available from the British Library

Library of Congress Cataloging-in-Publication Data
Goodman, Ed.
  New business : next steps : the all-in-one guide to managing, marketing and growing your small business / Ed Goodman and Ann Hawkins.
     pages cm
  Includes index.
  ISBN 978-1-292-01766-2 (print) -- ISBN 978-1-292-01768-6 (PDF) -- ISBN 978-1-292-01770-9 (ePub) -- ISBN978-1-292-01767-9 (eText)
  1. Small business--Management. 2. New business enterprises--Management. I. Hawkins, Ann. II. Title.
  HD62.7.G687 2015
  658.02'2--dc23
                           2014042817

10 9 8 7 6 5 4 3 2 1
19 18 17 16 15

Cover design by Two Associates
Arrow icon © alexwhite. Shutterstock

Print edition typeset in 9.5pt ITC Giovanni by 3
Printed by Ashford Colour Press Ltd, Gosport

NOTE THAT ANY PAGE CROSS REFERENCES REFER TO THE PRINT EDITION

Contents

About the authors

Ed Goodman is a business start-up mentor who's worked with over 10,000 start-ups to successfully build their knowledge of financial management, social media, networking and more. He has also delivered keynote presentations and workshops at large-scale seminars and exhibitions, including the MADE Festival, Business Start-Up Show, and other events at Earls Court, ExCel London and The National Space Centre. Through independent consultancy and mentoring, along with aligned partnerships, he has worked with multinational corporations including Barclays, Google, Sage, Intuit and more.

In 2012, Ed co-founded the Cambridge Business Lounge, a co-working space and support hub for start-ups and small businesses. He also regularly blogs on small business topics, including 'The A–Z Guide to Starting a Business', as well as being a contributor on the BBC, commercial radio, podcasts and other established business blogs.

You can find Ed on Twitter @edagoodman.

Ann Hawkins has spent a large part of her career asking questions about what makes businesses successful and encouraging business owners to use this information to create actionable plans to transform their own future.

Ann founded The Inspired Group in 2005 to encourage peer group learning for owners of small businesses and, through running Mastermind Groups, has developed unique insights into the challenges of starting and growing a business. As well as being a lively and much sought-after speaker and trainer, she can be seen in a number of interviews on YouTube.

Since 2010 Ann has been a regular presenter on *The Business Hub* radio show, 'the show that helps anyone in business succeed', and produced her own 26-part series of interviews for the show, 'The A–Z of Business Success'.

An early adopter of blogging and social media, Ann now owns and presents *The Social Media Show*, interviewing worldwide experts in this fast-changing arena and advising business owners on how to use radically different approaches to create resilient and often disruptive business models.

Always ready for an interesting conversation, you can find Ann on Twitter @AnnHawkins.

Acknowledgements

I'd like to thank all the contributors of this book who have brought their experiences to life with the sole aim of helping others flourish.

Thank you also to my friends and family who bring colour to my world and are a constant source of support and enthusiasm.

Finally, to my wonderful (and patient) wife Nicky, my partner in life and work, and to our two boys, Harrison and Oliver, who inspire me every day.

Ed

You know those book dedications that say, 'I owe thanks to too many people to mention'? Well, this is one of them.

The ideas in this book come from thousands of stories, interviews, conversations, presentations, talks and chats, so if you have been involved in any of those, you have my heartfelt thanks.

If you are one of the many people who have told me over the years, 'You should write a book', thank you, too. I finally did it.

If I have been absent from your life while I got it written, thank you for your patience, especially my long-suffering husband Andrew and son Adam for your unfailing, unflagging support, belief and love. (Did I tell you I'll be doing it all again soon?)

Ann

Publisher's acknowledgements

The figure on page 91 was created by Sam Johnston using OmniGroup's OmniGraffle and Inkscape (includes Computer.svg by Sasa Stefanovic), and is reproduced under the Creative Commons Licence (**http://creativecommons.org/licenses/by-sa/3.0/**).

We are grateful to Nordstrom, Inc. for permission to reproduce their Employee Handbook on pages 178–79.

How to get your own questions answered

In addition to all the great advice and tips in this book we want you to be able to get answers to your individual questions and to become part of the NBNS Community.

We have a website: **www.newbusinessnextsteps.com** where we'll add more resources and update the information in the book. You will also be able to download the tables in the book from the website so that you can use them as working documents, which we highly recommend. The arrow below will indicate which tables can be found online:

To ask questions and get support from other business owners as well as take part in scheduled live discussions, please join our Google Plus Community. Look for New Business Next Steps in the G+ community directory.

Many business owners say that isolation is a big problem and this is a great solution. You might be in business on your own but you don't have to do it alone!

Introduction

This book is written for owners of new and young businesses who want to grow their business to provide a good living and a good life for themselves.

Some businesses are started specifically with growth or 'scale' and a quick exit in mind, usually referred to as 'start-ups' and run by 'entrepreneurs'.

This book is for those who have started a business in order to make a living by doing something they love. Growth is important for survival but not the main reason for running the business. These are the vast majority of all business owners.

Specifically, it's written for the most vulnerable of those businesses, the ones that have got started but haven't yet got to the critical five-year anniversary.

In the UK, 99 per cent of all businesses are small (0–49 employees). The majority (62.6 per cent) are sole proprietorships. As well as financial investment, these businesses all require an emotional investment, an investment of hopes and dreams, and this is why it's important for more of them to succeed.

The track record for small businesses is grim:

▶ 50 per cent of new businesses fail within 12 months, with 90 per cent no longer trading after five years

▶ 10 per cent close involuntarily due to insolvency or bankruptcy

▶ 90 per cent cease trading voluntarily because the business is too weak, or not providing a satisfactory income or return for the owners.

Other studies have estimated that, during their formative couple of years, around 40 per cent of small businesses manage to trade profitably, around 30 per cent trade at break-even and 30 per cent trade while making continual losses (**www.gov.uk/government/statistics/announcements/ business-population-estimates-for-the-uk-and-regions-2014-edition**).

We've written this book because we want to change this trend.

Key reasons for business failure include:

▶ starting up for the wrong reasons

▶ lack of planning

▶ not anticipating the time and resources needed

▶ poor market understanding

▶ general incompetence

▶ not understanding cash flow

▶ lack of business or industry experience

▶ ignoring competitive threats

▶ being in the wrong location

▶ lack of entrepreneurial ability

▶ personal burn-out

▶ and, most crucially, poor financial awareness.

If you are the owner of a new or a young business, you will find tools and ideas to help you to grow your business in a way that suits you, that takes account of the way the world is changing and that helps to make the journey an exciting adventure instead of a constant struggle.

How this book is organised

Everyone who reads the book will have different levels of expertise. You may be an expert on marketing but looking for help with managing finances, or great at managing people but struggling with IT, so we've designed it so that you can dip in and go straight to what interests you most.

You'll find some expert opinions and some examples of good practice and we've included lots of case studies of young businesses that are succeeding. These business owners share what is working for them, how they overcome obstacles and what they are looking for in the future. They are not mega-stars, they are people just like you and there is no reason why you can't grow your business in the same way that they have.

You'll also find a section in each chapter called 'Next steps' that gives you a quick and practical way to take those important next steps to growth.

Even more importantly, we are going to be available and accessible to help you with your specific business growth. You can listen to more in-depth interviews, get more ideas and help and interact with us on the website that supports this book: **www.newbusinessnextsteps.com**

Ed and Ann

1

Managing the business

Most people start a business in order to do something that they love or to create a better lifestyle for themselves and their families. Very few people start a business because they want to 'manage' it but, invariably, as the business grows, that's what they end up doing.

In this chapter we're going to look at:

▶ the transition from starting to growing a business

▶ why purpose is important

▶ whether you are the right person to manage your business

▶ what success means to you

▶ setting and achieving goals.

There are two very different elements involved: the business itself which is an unfeeling entity that works on logic, and you, the business owner who, like all human beings, is a mass of contradictory emotions.

Most businesses will succeed but all too often the human being gets in the way of success.

Given the right foundation and a business owner that does the right things at the right time, most businesses will succeed, but all too often the human being, for all sorts of reasons, gets in the way of success.

The best possible scenario is when both you and the business are set up for success: that is what this chapter is all about.

When you started your business, why did you choose to provide that particular service or product? What was behind your decision? Something will have led you down a particular route that rewards you with more than money, and finding that is the start of defining your purpose.

In a famous TED Talk, Simon Sinek suggests that a business is more likely to succeed if we know *why* the business exists (**www.ted.com/talks/ simon_sinek_how_great_leaders_inspire_action**).

A business is more likely to succeed if we know *why* the business exists.

It's not enough to say our businesses exist to solve a problem for our customers. What we need to do is make it clear what we believe about the work we do, so that those who believe what we believe want to become our partners, not just our customers, suppliers or employees.

Tesco has recently had an epiphany. It discovered that a large number of its customers, suppliers and employees regarded the company as a predator. It has taken the decision to change the way it operates and, in the words of Matt Atkinson, past CEO, 'to rebuild the business to be a partner, not a predator' (David Cushman, *The 10 Principles of Open Business*, Palgrave Macmillan 2014). Why? Perhaps because in 2012 Tesco posted its first drop in profits in over 20 years and has recognised that, as the internet and social networks make customers and their views more powerful, the whole way businesses treat their customers needs to change.

The art of making partners of customers applies to all businesses and it starts with the passion of the business owner and the clearly stated purpose of the business. The idea of this is that we all know WHAT we do and, hopefully, HOW we do it but what has the most impact on attracting customers is WHY we do what we do.

An example of this is that even though Apple computers are more expensive than other PCs and have fewer software apps available to use on them, they are hugely popular. The reason is that people buy into the Apple vision and will pay more for a computer that reflects their values rather than make a purely logical decision.

In a traditional marketing message starting with the WHAT, Apple would say, 'We make great computers. They are beautifully designed and simple to use. Do you want to buy one?' Chances are you are not inspired by that. It does say what they do but it's still uninspiring. If Apple were to start with their WHY, they'd say, 'In everything we do, we believe in challenging the status quo and thinking differently. We do this by making our products beautifully designed and simple to use. Do you want to buy one?'

If you like the idea of challenging the status quo and thinking differently, you'll be queuing up to buy their products as soon as they're released. If not, no problem. The message is intended to attract Apple's target market, not just anybody. Any business can explain what it does; most can explain how they do it; but very few can clearly articulate WHY.

The reason WHY your business exists is not just to make money, quality products or services. Those are results. To discover your WHY, you need to get personal. WHY does your business exist? WHY does it do the things it does? And WHY should anyone care?

Knowing your WHY will help define your strategy, branding, marketing, products and services. It will help you to differentiate your business and rise above the competition.

In its simplest form, WHY is your purpose for creating the company.

▶ Sam Walton (Walmart) wanted to make quality goods affordable and available to rural USA.

▶ Herb Kellerman (SouthWest Airlines) wanted to take the stodginess out of air travel, and bring it to the common people.

▶ Bill Gates (Microsoft) had a vision of accessible information for all.

Each of these people had a clear vision of a better future. Their company was not created to make money; making money was simply a benefit of realising their visions. WHY taps into people's gut decisions.

A WHY is just a belief. That's all it is.

HOWs are the actions you take to realise that belief. WHATs are the results of those actions – everything you say and do: your products, services, marketing, culture and who you hire.

When someone asks, 'Why should I do business with you?' your answer should leave them in no doubt about what they can expect from you, and, just as importantly, what you will expect of them.

> Why does your business exist? What do you believe about its purpose that fills you with excitement and passion?
>
> ....
>
> ....
>
> ....

Why purpose is important

Google is a great example of a business with a purpose: with annual revenues of over $50 billion dollars, its purpose is the same one that it started out with: 'To organise the world's information and make it universally useful.' That purpose is supported by a set of principles that act as guidance on how Googlers – as members of staff are known – should behave in order to achieve that purpose:

1 Focus on the user and all else will follow.
2 It's best to do one thing really, really well.
3 Fast is better than slow.
4 Democracy on the web works.
5 You don't need to be at your desk to need an answer.
6 You can make money without doing evil.
7 There's always more information out there.
8 The need for information crosses all borders.
9 You can be serious without a suit.
10 Great just isn't good enough.

While Google's purpose has remained rock solid since it started in 2009, Yahoo, once their biggest rival, is now a pale shadow. Yahoo has had several mission statements since it started in 2007, but it often changes and is not universally understood by employees, suppliers or customers.

Walking the talk has never been more important. In 2012, Yahoo's revenue was less than 10 per cent of Google's. That's how important purpose is. Giving people information isn't enough. What we need is to connect emotionally and not by what we say but by what we do. Walking the talk has never been more important.

> Would your customers, employees and suppliers get a clear idea of what to expect by reading your purpose statement?
>
> ....
>
> ....
>
> ....

Purpose is not a mission statement

A mission statement is often used as an internal guide for formulating strategies. It should spell out the company's overall goal. In theory it should be the same as the purpose and the WHY but too often mission statements are bland, have nothing to connect them emotionally to the customer and fail to say anything about WHY the company exists or its beliefs. A mission statement that is written with shareholders or investors in mind is not likely to have an emotional connection with customers.

This is an example of a purpose statement from Jon Torrens, a presentation and public-speaking coach specialising in the computer games industry:

'I believe that when you give a presentation it should be because you want to change something. Becoming a superb presenter gives you the power to change hearts, minds, opinions, perceptions, motivation, desires, behaviour, spending patterns and more. I am the Shinobi of the speaking world, eliminating boring presentations and allowing true influencers to shine.'

Re-thinking purpose

Corporate greed has caused a lot of consumers to re-think what really matters in how they live and work and how they want to be treated. Technology is allowing people to collaborate in ways not previously possible and this means that we are in one of the most exciting times to be in business.

Companies like Honda, Harley-Davidson, Patagonia, Whole Foods, Yeo Valley Farms, Zappos, Costco and many more are proving that companies based on love, joy, authenticity and soul are becoming the ultimate value creators. They're not doing it because it's politically correct or the flavour of the moment *but because they are proving that it's the only path to long-term competitive advantage.*

New Balance shoes, started by an English immigrant to America over a century ago, was founded to help people have healthy feet and a healthy life. Its slogan is, 'Connect with yourself – achieve New Balance'. Compare this to Nike's slogan 'Just do it', and compare the adverts: a man running along a mountain track overlooking a shimmering sea. The New Balance advert says, 'The shortest distance between two points is not the point', whereas a similar Nike advert is all about effort and, most importantly, winning.

New Balance sees itself as a shoe-*making* company and keeps all its manufacturing in the USA. Nike is a shoe *marketing* company, outsourcing manufacturing to the cheapest supplier and spending huge amounts of money on celebrity endorsements.

Despite this, and the fact that New Balance pays higher wages, its market share and profits keep rising whereas Nike, Adidas and Reebok are all experiencing declining sales and market share.

How much time should you spend managing your business?

Most owners of young businesses admit to working 60 hours a week. Until the business is big enough to employ specialists the recommended time split is:

▶ marketing: 55 per cent (33 hours)

▶ making (delivering a service): 35 per cent (21 hours)

▶ managing: 10 per cent (6 hours).

Are you the right person to manage your business?

Expert opinion Alexey Manichenko, Chief Executive of Skylark Learning Limited

 Alexey Manichenko became the CEO of Umnitsa in 2007. The company was founded by his father in Russia in 1999. When Alexey decided to move to the UK in 2012 he hired a Managing Director to take over the running of the company. The company develops, publishes and distributes international award-winning book and card sets, learning games and digital programs for children.

Alexey is currently the Chief Executive of Skylark Learning Limited in Cambridge and we asked him about his experience of hiring an MD to run his family-owned business.

What was the hardest part about deciding to appoint a Managing Director in your place? The issue of trust. For the first time, all day-to-day decisions in the business were to be made by someone who was not from the family and who had nothing to lose, ultimately, except his or her job. We, on the other hand, risked the business that we had been building for 13 years by that time and which was the primary source of income for all the family.

Did you get any resistance about making this decision? Yes, a lot. My parents started the business and they invested heavily into my education and, of course, they trusted me like they could trust no one else. My wife and I decided to move to the UK for the sake of our children, and their grandparents understood this, for which we are grateful. They trusted me to have prepared everything for a smooth transition and to maintain a degree of control over the company after the move. We had a very honest discussion of the risks involved and outlined a couple of 'worst-case scenarios'. We were psychologically ready for a temporary dip in the 'learning curve' for the business for the sake of our family's longer-term goals.

Do you think the business has suffered because you are not there to manage it? I am honestly not sure. The company's turnover had always grown

▶

year-on-year, although the pace of that growth had been decreasing from +130 per cent in 2006 down to +15 per cent in 2011. The increasing intensity of the competition and no revolutionary breakthroughs of the sort that propelled our growth in the early years were some of the reasons. In 2012 we achieved 25 per cent growth for the year. I left my position as CEO in July 2012. In 2013 the company grew only 4 per cent, but 2014, fingers crossed, has shown a very different, very positive dynamic.

I do believe this to be the short-term learning curve dip that people say is inevitable when you radically change something in the way you operate. What has been happening in the business after the initial 18 months of the MD's tenure gives us hope for a much brighter future. I think handing over may turn out to be a very good thing long term. The management team has been learning a lot, being fully responsible for their own decisions without daily supervision or guidance from the owners for the first time. I hope they can achieve things in the future that will make us all very proud.

Are there any issues of leadership or loyalty that you have had to deal with? The MD, her team, I, my family and all the 100 employees of the company had to learn a lot. We had to establish boundaries of trust and authority as we went. It proved impossible for us to envisage everything prior to the handing over.

I started my succession planning in late 2007. Impressed by Jim Collins' *Built To Last*, I was eager to create systems that solve problems rather than solving them myself. Maria Tsurkan, the eventual MD, joined the company in 2006. In 2007 she was head of marketing and together with other managers attended a training course I designed on how to run the company day-to-day. In 2009 Maria was selected to start and run our first subsidiary and was appointed the first-ever MD of our Moscow office. In 2010 we started a twice-yearly internal training programme for our managers which we continue to this day. In 2011 Maria and four more colleagues started their MBAs, heavily sponsored by the company. By the time I had to choose a successor in 2012, Maria had had experience of managing an autonomous division of the company, all the training we could think of at the time and, most importantly, trust and respect of the team. We both thought we were ready.

The hardest part for me in what followed was to learn to let go. I needed all my courage to just let Maria decide without taking things back in my own hands. Often I saw an obvious way to go when she hesitated. The company could probably move faster. The flip side of that would be that she and her team would learn less, and in the long term it would be more dangerous for the company.

What are the particular problems that you face because of the distance?
We speak with Maria twice a week over Skype. She uses me as a coach and advisor, I use these meetings to better understand how she feels and what priorities she currently has.

We have a formal 'Board' meeting once a month (they used to be weekly until only three months ago). There are reports that we all receive monthly, weekly and daily (this one is sent automatically by our management information system). I try to go to Russia myself for a week every two months or so.

Of course, without being physically there, it is impossible to know exactly what is going on. But then, do I need to know everything? There are, I think, just two important things to do to keep calm. The first is to set systems for regularly getting objective factual information on how the business is doing. The other is to maintain regular face-to-face communication (which can be done over Skype) for keeping and developing trust.

What advice would you give to people who try to do everything themselves instead of delegating to others? I think of it this way. Being a manager is a choice. It is the only profession where you can produce more than you are capable of as an individual. A hospital manager will help a lot more people in a year than an individual doctor can see during their entire career. If you do not delegate, you are not a manager.

Now, should a company owner be a manager? Not always and not necessarily. If you run your company and there is more than you in it, then yes, you have to be a manager.

If you are a manager and you do not delegate everything you can, you do not do your own job, which is building the company, developing people, setting direction, providing feedback and, of course, learning. These things require all

▶

the time you've got. If you are busy doing something that someone else in the company could do, you are wasting your company's most expensive resource – your time and energy.

Based on your experience, what advice would you give to business owners who feel that their business might benefit from hiring someone else to manage it? Start early. Learn about it, speak to people who have done it and make your own strategy. I'd recommend appointing someone from the company, as opposed to hiring an outsider. The risks are much lower. When you don't have good internal candidates or when you have an outstanding external candidate, I'd invite the external person to take a mid-level management position to start with, and later promote them to run the business if they prove themselves and if you build enough trust for going further together.

Find ways to make sure the candidate has intimate knowledge of your business before you step away. They should know the people and the way things are done and why, the market and where it is headed, the customers and their needs. All this can be achieved when you have time and a plan. Make your candidates learn on the job. Give them hard tasks and make them do your job by increasing chunks. It's the best way to learn, and it will give you opportunities to assess their real progress, not just how they absorb information, but also what they actually do with it.

Technical knowledge can be learned. Trust can be built. But only when you have time. Start early.

What does success mean for you?

Success means different things to everyone. There will always be people you consider to be doing better or not as well as you. Comparing yourself to others loses any meaning when you know exactly what YOU want to achieve.

Success is more likely if your business goals are closely aligned to the way you want to live your life. Running a business just for the money does work, but it's even better if you can not only enjoy the process but get satisfaction and pride as well as a financial return.

Here's an exercise that helps to define this:

(a) What kind of person do you want to be and what kind of life do you want to live?

(b) What do you have to do to be that person and live that life?

(c) When you become that person and live that life, what will you have?

Here's an example of an answer:

(a) I want to be fulfilled and prosperous, generous and popular, loved by my family and friends and respected by my peers. I want to live a life full of adventure, using my skills and talents and making a difference to other people.

(b) I need to build a business that I am proud of, that satisfies me and provides me with an income of £xxx a year. I need to travel to wherever I'm needed and connect with the people who will benefit from my skills and talents.

(c) I will have peace of mind, security and the ability to help others.

The importance of your beliefs on your success

Beliefs influence our behaviour. Belief is an ever-important aspect of creating a successful business. If you can imagine it but you truly don't believe it, then achieving it will be a struggle. Your worry, doubt and uncertainty will act as a barrier that prohibits you from reaching your goals.

Most people doubt themselves. For some it's occasionally and for others it's often. We also tend to put other people on a pedestal. The funny thing is that the people we admire, who we think have got it made, often doubt themselves as much as everyone else. We all have problems, insecurities and challenges. What makes

The more you believe in yourself, the more likely you are to accomplish your goals.

the difference is how we handle them. Belief is the best tool! The more you believe in yourself and your abilities, the more likely you are to accomplish your goals.

> Write a list of why you believe you will have the life and business of
> your dreams. Include everything – skills, values, personal characteristics,
> philosophy, experience, talents and anything else that you think is relevant.

While you're thinking about your beliefs, check to see if any of them are really wants. It's good to want things and fight for them, but it's important to check that your beliefs are not getting in the way of what you want.

Make a decision to succeed

This is the very foundation of a successful business. So many people just jump into their business and rush around trying to get clients. They don't stop and actually make that decision or that commitment to build a successful business no matter what it takes. They are just checking things out, putting out feelers, and seeing what works or if it will work without ever really committing to making their business a success.

Without that decision, that commitment, you will not get through the difficult times.

Building a business is not easy. Being fully committed to doing what it takes gives you more focus, clarity, purpose, inspiration and motivation. Let's face it; you will have to overcome obstacles! If it was easy to build a successful and profitable business, everyone would be a business owner.

Your decision will remind you of the reasons why you became a business owner and why you want to succeed in your business.

A decision comes before we set our goals because unless we actually decide to make it happen there is no goal in the world that will make us go forward to achieve it.

Sometimes you need to make a decision about what you don't want in order to get to what you do want.

Setting and achieving goals

You may be thinking, 'I've set goals before and not achieved them so what's the point?' There are many systems and methods of goal setting and many myths and legends too.

What makes a good goal?

SMART goals, big hairy goals, goals that excite you, goals that scare you, goals that are realistic and achievable.

If someone else has done it – chances are, you can too.

If no one else has done it yet, it means there are no rules!

Your goals and values must be in accord. One of the main reasons that we don't achieve our goals is that the goal is in conflict with other things in our lives. For example, having a goal of building a business with many branches in different parts of the country or in other countries will probably involve spending a lot of time away from home. If one of your most important roles is that of a parent and your goal for that role is to always be home for supper or to help with homework, then your business goal and your life goal will be in conflict.

List all the roles you play in your life, e.g. parent, child, sibling, friend, business owner, employer, employee, community worker, volunteer, teacher, supporter, artist, gardener, carer.

. . . .

. . . .

Take the three most important roles that you have identified and write a goal for each one for the coming year.

Role	Goal
1	
2	
3	

Now look at how you plan to achieve your goals:

A RESULT-oriented goal would be to earn £xxx by a particular date. This can sometimes result in embarking on a plan of action that you hate and you have to grit your teeth every day to move closer to your goal.

A PROCESS-oriented goal would be to make xx number of calls or write xx number of proposals and to sell so many products or so many hours of your time every day. Because you focus on the process, you are more likely to choose one that you enjoy and can turn into a new life habit. An important point about this is that, however much you want the result, if you hate the process you are unlikely to succeed. Finding a process that is enjoyable is the best way to achieve any goal.

Make sure that each goal is in line with your personal values.

Don't kid yourself by setting goals you're unlikely to achieve – that is just setting yourself up for failure – but don't undersell yourself either. Making the goal too easy won't give you any satisfaction.

Dig down into any doubts or worries and make sure that the way you plan to achieve each goal is in line with your personal values.

This is really about unearthing your big lifetime goals and the things that might be holding you back from fulfilling your potential, using your skills and talents in accordance with your personal values and getting closer to leading a life of integrity and satisfaction. If your lifetime goals are clear, making short-term goals for the coming year and every future year that will take you closer to them will provide satisfaction in itself.

From the goals you've identified for each role, choose the ones that will make the most difference to your life. Keep checking back and revising the list until you have a list that thrills and excites you. If your list causes you doubts and worries, dig up the reasons. Be honest with yourself and if you really can't see yourself achieving a particular goal, cross it out and replace it. There is no 'should' about this list. It's about what you truly 'want' and no one's judgement is involved except your own.

Identifying your top three goals will give you a clear focus and a way to get started. It will also help with day-to-day decision making. Every time you are faced with a dilemma about what action to take ask yourself, 'Will this take me closer or further away from my most important goals this year?'

This is a good time to reflect that no one can make changes without affecting the people around them and the environment in which they live. Identify who will be most affected by the changes you want to make and make sure they are aware, in agreement and, ideally, supportive.

How can you make sure you achieve your top goals?

Just writing down goals will not get results. Just making a plan will not get results. Just thinking positive thoughts will not get results.

Consistent action coupled with a firm belief is most likely to get the results you want but even then, circumstances outside of your control may influence what happens. You can't control what happens but you can control how you react to it.

Your plan to achieve your goals needs to be a living breathing part of every second of your life. Every decision you make will take you nearer or further away from achieving your goals. Achieving your goals is not something you do as well as doing everything else in your life. Achieving your goals is about the way you live every moment. If your goals are consistent with your values and the roles you play in your life, the changes you make will lead naturally to the end you have in mind.

Planning to achieve your goals

Most things happen without a plan. Many of them are good things: friendships, falling in love, finding great music, food or art, or things that make you laugh. Spontaneity and serendipity are important. However, if you want to achieve particular goals it means making space in your life for what really matters and taking action by doing things you enjoy.

> For each goal, write down three action points that you will do within the next month:
>
> Goal 1: . . . .
>
> . . . .

> Goal 2:...
> ....
> Goal 3:...
> ....

When you create good, sustainable habits that you enjoy, you'll end up with a life you are proud of.

You don't have to do it alone

It's been said you are a combination of the five people you spend most time with. Look at the people who you hang out with all of the time. Your eating habits, overall health, wealth and levels of success are all likely to be similar. What does this mean for you? It means you are who you hang out with. This means that if you want things to be different, you probably need to associate with different people.

There are four crucial people that you need to have on your team in order to create the success that you want:

▶ **Mentor:** This is someone you know who has had success in the areas in which you want to be successful. If you're unfit and want to be healthy and strong, find somebody who used to be unfit and is now healthy and strong and find out how they did it. (Remember you have to like the process or it won't work for you.) If you want to earn more, learn to sing, open a shop, win a medal, find somebody who has had that experience and learn everything you can about how they did it.

▶ **Buddy:** This is someone who is struggling with the same things, working on the same stuff as you. When you have a bad day, this person knows exactly how you feel. Because you're both striving for the same goals, you have somebody to bounce ideas around with, share triumphs and struggles with. Caution: don't take the buddy support as far as going down the plughole together. Understanding it's hard doesn't mean you support each other in giving up.

▶ **Student:** The best way to get better at something is to teach it to somebody else. If you think you need to be an expert in order to teach, think of expertise on a scale of 1–100. If you're a 5 you can help out the 1–4s. Find somebody that needs help, maybe a co-worker or friend who wants to do what you're doing, and teach them how to get started. As you get better and learn from your mentor, you can then compare and share this with your buddy and then help teach it to your student.

▶ **Cheerleader:** This is the person who will always be in your corner, cheering you on. They'll believe in you more than you believe in yourself, have high expectations, keep you on your toes, push you outside of your comfort zone, make you try new things, not let you settle for less, dust you off when you fall and push you back out there.

Next steps

▶ Write the purpose of your business. Use emotional words that express your passion and your beliefs and that will help you to connect with people who believe what you believe about your business.

▶ Write your definition of success.

▶ Decide on your three major goals for the next 12 months.

▶ Gather your team: your mentor, your buddy, your cheerleader and your student.

▶ Taking all this into account, write down your business objectives for the next:

   ▶ three months

   ▶ six months

   ▶ 12 months

   ▶ longer term.

Klaxon

klaxon™

Andy Bargery, Managing Director of Klaxon, talked to us about starting his business in 2006. The business currently has three full-time employees and a pool of freelancers, including an ex-director, that give it both flexibility and a range of specialist skills.

How was the business funded at the start? I started out using my savings to buy a laptop and rent some desk space. I managed to secure my first two paying clients within a week which allowed me to get going without taking on any debt. Thankfully the fees started flowing in before I ran out of savings.

What prompted you to start your business? I had been working as an Account Director for a PR agency running accounts for big technology clients including Cisco and HP. I was also the General Manager, which meant I had gained a lot of insight into the workings of the agency: finance, human resources and internal communications. This meant I was also involved when the agency's owner put it up for sale and ultimately exited the business. I felt this experience had given me enough understanding and experience to set up on my own.

What talents did you bring to the business? I have always been quite entre-preneurial, setting up my first business in high school with an unofficial tuck shop. This interest led me on to a business degree where I also found a natural fit with the marketing courses, where I was able to engage the creative side of my brain. I then worked in marketing and communication roles for a couple of multinationals which helped me to decide that I preferred the cut and thrust of working in small companies and subsequently I joined a small PR agency as its first full-time employee.

At what point did you feel that your business was established? I can't say I have ever felt my business is truly established. Every day I learn something new, or face a new challenge servicing clients and running the business. My gut feeling is, I will only feel it is established when I achieve my goal of a successful exit.

What has been your biggest business challenge? Finding the right people to join the team is always a big risk and challenge, not just from an employee point of view but also finding partners and advisors. I have hired poorly in the past, which was a painful and costly experience – our first employee spilt water over her laptop within the first two weeks, dropped and broke her smartphone and then ultimately left, taking a client with her.

What were the major challenges affecting the growth of the business? The marketing industry is hugely dynamic and the pace of change is incredible. New technology changes the rules all of the time and keeping on top of that is almost a full-time job. This has created a sector where competition is phenomenal. Where previously there was a clear distinction between marketing, PR and advertising, now technological advances means all are very much playing in the same space. Looking inwards we need to make sure our housekeeping is up to date. Keeping on top of the day-to-day business functions such as cash flow, invoicing and our own marketing is something we are always working hard to achieve.

I used to be a lot less strict on the cash flow, but I now know the only way we can grow and achieve our business objectives is to have absolute clarity on our cash position. Without this insight there is no way I can make the decisions that will enable us to grow.

What other challenges did you have? Initially I found it hard to define our target marketing and ideal customer. I used to chase after every client and piece of business, particularly where I thought the work would lead to cash flow that covered the overheads. Now I look at it a bit differently. Our business development focuses on market segments where we have the most experience and good credentials. I qualify prospective clients based on their knowledge of and ability to work with a marketing agency; otherwise we spend too much time educating clients that ultimately reduces our profit margins.

How did you overcome these issues? It took advice from a business development professional and a business coach to realise we had a problem. Once I understood the need to target, we shifted the focus of our business development, changed our messaging, targeted our communications, and unsurprisingly the sales pipeline started to look a lot healthier. This is ironic really as this is the same advice we give to our clients who define their target market as anyone. I understand that it's not uncommon for plumbers to have leaky taps!

Who have you got support from? I work with a business coach who provides regular input that shapes our strategy, but also helps with the detail too, keeping me accountable to the actions I commit to delivering. I strongly recommend every business owner finds someone external to the business who can provide this support.

I also have a network of advisors including an accountant, solicitor and an employment law specialist to turn to when I have specific needs or requirements.

Perhaps the biggest support comes from my family who understand that running your own business comes with extra responsibilities and stresses.

Have you had any business failures that you have learned from? Before I started Klaxon, I joined a team of friends that set up a nightclub promotion venture. It was very exciting and we had a great time. We rented a famous London night club, hired DJs and created a brand and promotions, but ultimately the venture failed. Some of the reasons for this are that we didn't have a business plan, the product wasn't differentiated in a crowded market place. We were also a group of friends, which was a recipe for disaster when it came to making tough decisions.

We also regularly test new ideas for how to develop our business with new products and services. Some ideas work and some fail, but each improves our knowledge and ability to consult clients.

What is your vision for the business? I want to build an agency that delivers marketing campaigns in a measured environment that really make a difference to our clients. I have developed a team of experienced and highly skilled marketers to achieve this. We can help our clients to understand their target audience, build a business strategy and marketing plan that drives engagement with those audiences, and ultimately converts them into customers. I have an exit strategy in mind, which helps me to set objectives for the business.

What was the most useful piece of advice you had when you started? I don't recall being given any particularly good advice when I started out. I do remember being told many times how much hard work is involved in running your own business. This is without a doubt true. It requires a lot of work to run a business and at times it requires tough decision making, but ultimately it is very rewarding.

What tip would you offer someone who is making the transition from starting out to growing their business? Create a network of skilled advisors to draw upon and get to grips with your finances. As your business grows you will need to have a very clear picture of what's happening with your cash, it is the lifeblood of your business and without knowing your cash flow there is no way you can make the decisions you need to in order to grow.

2

Managing growth

There are two types of business owner: those that complain because the business isn't growing fast enough and those that complain because it's growing too quickly.

Managing growth can be tricky and just as many businesses flounder because they have taken on too much as those who don't have enough work.

In this chapter we're going to look at:

► choosing the right growth strategy

► creating a growth plan

► formal company structures

► traditional and open businesses

► analysing business potential

► managing risks

► financing growth.

When you start a business and you've done every role in it at some point, it can be very hard to let go of managing all the details. Managing growth effectively is all about making sure you have the resources to deliver as demand increases, and the time to spot any potential problems before they become an issue.

Managing growth is about making sure you have the resources to deliver as demand increases.

Choosing the right growth strategy

There are several ways to grow a business other than expanding organically as sales and profits increase. Choosing the right one will depend on the type of business you own, your available resources, and how much money, time and effort you want to invest. Several of the options listed below will need the involvement of experienced accountants and lawyers and the accompanying expenses that this entails.

1   **Buy another business.** Known as an 'acquisition', there are several reasons why this is a good idea. Buying a bankrupt or loss-making business that you believe you can turn around not only guarantees a good price and a way to move into new markets but has tax advantages too. Buying a profitable business that is capable of accelerated growth gives you an immediate income stream to offset the cost of buying and can also bring economies of scale, talented staff and new ideas.

2   **Merge with another business.** This is usually done when two similar businesses decide they could be more successful as one and can be achieved by swapping shares or by more complicated payment options.

3   **Open in another location.** Physical expansion needs careful research, planning and especially financial planning as it could involve borrowing money for mortgages or rent, extra stock and staff. You need:

   ▶ a consistent bottom-line profit and steady growth over the past few years

   ▶ seamless systems and processes that will transfer to the new location

   ▶ key people to run in more than one location

   ▶ a complete business plan for a new location

   ▶ to choose the new location based on what's best for your business, not what you can afford.

4   **Franchise.** The early stages can be very expensive and involve a lot of time and effort in legal preparation before you even get to the stage of selling franchises. However, when people have a vested interest in operating what essentially becomes their own business within your framework, they put more effort in and are generally successful because you've already proved that the model works.

5   **Licensing.** This represents a way to move a brand into new businesses without making a major investment in new processes or manufacturing facilities. In a well-run licensing programme, the owner maintains control over the brand image and how it's portrayed and reaps the benefit in additional revenue (royalties), but also in exposure in new channels. Examples might include:

▶ a branded business service or process that is licensed to consultants

▶ a brand of gardening tools licensed into a business making gardening gloves or boots

▶ a restaurant chain licensing a frozen food manufacturer to market ready meals under its brand.

This strategy also needs investment in legal processes and contracts but has the advantage of relatively small upfront risk. By licensing it is possible to try new markets or new countries with a smaller upfront investment than by building and staffing your own operations.

6   **Form an alliance.** Aligning yourself with a similar type of business can be a powerful way to expand quickly. An example might be a business that sells fitness training to new mothers aligning itself with a business that sells baby buggies as they both have the same target market but different products. Working out complimentary commission rates benefits everyone.

7   **Diversify.** Diversifying is an excellent growth strategy, as it allows you to have multiple streams of income that can often fill seasonal voids and, of course, increase sales and profit margins. While this can seem very attractive, it's important that the core business isn't neglected while you pursue something new and shiny! Examples of diversifying include:

▶ a property developer might become a conference speaker, writer and TV presenter

▶ a dairy farm could branch out into making related products such as cheese, yoghurt or ice cream

▶ a massage therapist might sell oils and gift packs or online stress relief programmes

▶ a restaurant might sell their own line of salad dressings, sauces or cookbooks in supermarkets

▶ a sports equipment retailer could offer specialist coaching services.

8 **Target other markets.** You may have chosen one target market to get your business going and to simplify marketing but that doesn't mean you can't expand into other markets once you're established and making money.

Growing organically

This is the most popular choice of most small businesses, but it works much better if you have a well thought-out plan. If you start a growth phase in your business it is usually because you've done something right. A new product or service has been launched, marketing has been effective, the sales are coming in and you're delivering efficiently. This cycle will continue for a while, but as you take on more customers to feed the growth, you will at some point reach the limit of your business capacity. You might run out of human power, business resources or the ability to manage operational issues effectively.

Your overall plan for the business is a crucial factor in how you handle a growth phase.

Your overall plan for the business is a crucial factor in how you handle this. If you are likely to seek capital to expand, having an experienced management team in place is very attractive to investors but then you need to adjust your behaviour to suit the new structure.

One way to do this is to choose the way you will measure growth over the next three years and chart this out. For example:

Year	Turnover	Profit	Number of employees	Number of locations	Number of products

List the major tasks that you need to do in order to get the growth you've identified then decide how this will be done, who will be responsible for getting each task done and by when. The plan could look something like this:

Year one: Hire two engineers, launch a new product, and attract an investor

What, who, when	Action	Action	Action	Action	Action
Hire two engineers	Prepare job description and advertise	Interview	Appoint and induct	Bring up to speed	Review productivity
Who					
When					
Launch new product					
Who					
When					
Attract an investor					
Who					
When					

The formal structure

A growing company needs a manager with the commitment to be a large-scale leader. For many business owners this may be a role they didn't anticipate. If you started your business in order to do something you love, you may find that the business of managing growth isn't what you like or are suited to.

The interview with Alexey Manichenko in the previous chapter shows how it can be an advantage to bring in someone else to manage the business, but some business owners find they enjoy adapting to the new role. Whatever arrangement suits you, you are likely to have to change the formal structure of the business.

The following table highlights the pros and cons of three different types of structure:

Structure	Pros	Cons
Sole trader (described as any business owned by one person)	It's all yours; the control, decisions and net profits.	The primary negative has to be liability. In the eyes of the law, the business and the sole trader running it, are one and the same. Therefore, if the business runs into debt, the owner is liable. The worst case scenario is that your personal assets (your car, savings, even your house) are at risk.
Partnership	The main advantage of a partnership over a sole trader is the shared rewards (and risks). This allows one partner's strengths to complement another's. For example, if a restaurateur was in partnership with someone with a business background, one could concentrate on providing the food and service, and the other on handling the finances.	One of the major disadvantages of partnerships is taxation. The current laws mean that if the partnership (and the partners) brings in more than a certain level, they are subject to greater levels of personal taxation than they would be in a limited company. This means that in most cases setting up a limited company would be more beneficial as the taxation laws are more favourable.
Private Limited Company (Ltd)	The primary advantage to setting up a Limited Liability Company is just that: the limited liability. This means the Company's shareholders will only be liable for any debt the company accrues according to the levels of their own investment and no more. Unlike sole traders, no other personal assets are at risk. This can provide a comfortable feeling of security for investors in the Company.	Creating a Private Limited Company isn't expensive, and easy if you instruct an accountant or formations company to set it up for you. The main downside is increased paperwork, as there are more complex rules governing the accounts and bookkeeping of limited companies than for sole traders.

Other options include:

▶ **Public Limited Company (PLC).** As with a Private Limited Company, a PLC has limited liability. Its main difference is in the stock of the company, which can be acquired by anyone and holders are only limited to potentially lose the amount paid for the shares.

▶ **Co-operative.** Co-operative businesses are owned and run by and for their members, whether they are customers, employees or residents. The integrated business structure, allows its members to share the profits, liabilities and decision making authority.

▶ **Social enterprise.** Social enterprises are businesses that trade to tackle social problems, improve communities, people's life chances, or the environment. They make their money from selling goods and services in the open market, but they reinvest their profits back into the business or the local community.

If you attract people into your business by offering them shares instead of, or as well as, a director role, these have very different implications. For example, under the Companies Acts, some of the key decisions, such as changing the company's articles, can only be made by shareholders. However, the differences are much more than that, as well as having legal implications. Company law dictates that some actions must be made by shareholders, some by directors, and some by directors with the shareholders' permission. You can employ directors to make the day-to-day decisions of a company, controlling meetings and strategic developments, but it's the shareholders who hold the ultimate source of power.

The main documents you'll need when the shareholders and/or directors change within a business are:

▶ **Shareholders' Agreement.** The most important aspect of this agreement, for any shareholder, is that it protects their rights and ensures that all shareholders are treated fairly. This is a detailed arrangement between a company's shareholders which lays out how the company should be operated, the direction it should take, as well as the shareholders' rights and obligations. Other legal information in the Shareholders' Agreement includes the regulation of the shareholders' relationship, management of the company, ownership of shares and privileges and protection of shareholders.

▶ **Articles of Association.** The government defines the Articles of Association as 'rules about running the company that shareholders and "officers" (directors or company secretary) have to agree to. For example, rules about how decisions that affect the company must be made and the role of shareholders in those decisions'. There are standard articles which can be used, to ensure you're compliant, but often companies decide to write their own. If you do, hire a company law solicitor to give them the once over, to ensure they are written within the law.

These changes should ideally be made with the advice of an accountant and, in the case of the Shareholders' Agreement, a lawyer, as they all have tax or legal implications.

Traditional or open structure?

Most new businesses have a very flat structure with a lot of cross-over of responsibilities. Communication is fast and easy and decision making isn't a problem, but as the business grows it typically gets organised into departments, each with its own manager, and this means that communication and decision making can slow down and get caught in all sorts of internal hold-ups.

However, a number of companies are actively staying with a flat structure, with no managers, bringing a democratic or sociocratic approach to the way they work and, in doing so, proving that they are better places to work, give better service to customers, work better with suppliers and make more money.

Other factors are coming into play to challenge the traditional approach to growing a business. Technology is making it possible for businesses to be 'networked' using enabling platforms. A great example of this is blur Group, which connects businesses with more than 32,000 expert service providers in more than 140 countries and has only 50 employees. Another platform-based business is Airbnb, which connects over 600,000 property owners with people looking for cheap lodgings. With almost zero operating costs, the business owners have become billionaires in a very short space of time. Another example of this style of business model is Uber, which makes mobile apps that connect passengers with drivers of vehicles for hire and ridesharing services and is now expanding into other services and products.

Dubbed 'the sharing economy', hundreds of millions of people are already transferring parts of their economic lives to this new business model. They are making and sharing their own information, entertainment, green energy and 3D-printed products at near zero marginal cost. Besides sharing homes, cars, clothes and other household items via social media sites, there are also redistribution clubs and co-operatives at low or near zero marginal cost.

Non-profit bike-sharing services are a good example of the new sharing economy. About 132 million bicycles were sold around the world in 2012, with revenues exceeding $33 billion. But now, an increasing number of young people are deciding they don't need to own bikes; they are perfectly happy to have access to shared bikes, and pay only for the time they use them. As millennials shift from bike ownership to bike-sharing services, revenues are likely to plummet in the bicycle manufacturing industry because more people will be sharing fewer bikes.

The internet is changing the course of economic history.

These kinds of phenomena are going to continue to spread in the years ahead. As hundreds of millions of people shift large parts of their economic activity to the internet, they will change the course of economic history.

> Is your business fixed to a particular location, offering personal face-to-face service with staff who work from a specific location?
>
> If so, is there a service you can create that could be offered as an online addition to your offering?

An example of this might be an IT support company that is moving more of its services to remote monitoring of customers' equipment, more cloud care services and help desk services for customers. This means that the number of face-to-face transactions is reduced but that customers still get excellent and much faster service.

Analysing business potential

A systems-driven business allows you to measure performance data against the processes. For example, you can see how many widgets were made last week against target, or how many installations failed in the last month. These analytics provide a check to verify that the process was followed, or a record of what went wrong.

Even when you have set up the systems, developed your management team and implemented quality control procedures, you must still pay attention to the numbers.

So, let's imagine that sales are going well. Your revenue is growing at an incredible rate but your finance instinct tells you something isn't right. On the face of it growth is good and you've been hiring, but hidden expenses – such as discretionary purchases your staff might be making on company credit cards, or even just not reviewing your suppliers' costs on a regular basis – have started to outstrip your revenue growth. The statistics will tell you where the problem is, let you analyse it and then you can create a system with the right procedures to fix the issue before the situation affects your business adversely.

Statistics will tell you where the problem is, let you analyse it and then you can create a system to fix it.

This is exactly the type of problem that kills fast-growing businesses and why it is always necessary for the business owner to keep a check on the numbers:

'I realised that to grow my business, I needed to let go and focus on what I do best – strategic planning and business development – and rely on experts and advisers for some of the other details. I started to learn how to hire smart. I brought in a part-time financial officer who told me I had to get away from accounting. I hired a part-time controller but didn't trust him at first, so I had him work on a duplicate system for a year. Once I learned how to effectively delegate, our growth skyrocketed at a rate of 30% to 40% each year.'

Lisa Firestone, president and owner of Managed Care Advisors,
www.businessinsider.com/small-business-lessons-learned-2014-1?op=1

PEST analysis

You've probably heard of a SWOT analysis (Strengths, Weaknesses, Opportunities, Threats), but before doing a SWOT analysis it can be useful to do a PEST analysis first.

The PEST analysis is a useful tool for understanding market growth or decline, and as such the position, potential and direction for a business.

PEST is an acronym for Political, Economic, Social and Technological factors, which are used to assess the market for a business. The PEST analysis headings are a framework for reviewing a situation, and can also, like a SWOT analysis, be used to review a strategy or position, the direction, marketing proposition or an idea.

The basic PEST analysis includes four factors:

▶ **Political factors.** Look at the degree to which the government intervenes in the economy. Specifically, political factors include areas such as tax policy, labour law, environmental law, trade restrictions, tariffs, and political stability. Political factors may also include goods and services that the government may or may not want to provide or be provided.

▶ **Economic factors.** Include economic growth, interest rates, exchange rates and the inflation rate. These factors have major impacts on how businesses operate and make decisions. For example, interest rates affect a firm's cost of capital and therefore to what extent a business grows and expands. Exchange rates affect the costs of exporting goods and the supply and price of imported goods in an economy.

▶ **Social factors.** Include the cultural aspects like health consciousness, population growth rate, age distribution, career attitudes and emphasis on safety. Trends in social factors affect the demand for a company's products and how that company operates. For example, an aging population may imply a smaller and less cost-effective workforce. Companies may change various management strategies to adapt to these social trends (such as recruiting older workers).

▶ **Technological factors.** Include technological aspects such as Research and Development activity, automation, technology incentives and the rate of technological change. They can determine barriers to entry, minimum efficient production level and influence outsourcing decisions. Furthermore, technological shifts can affect costs, quality, and lead to innovation.

Expanding the analysis adds:

▶ **Legal factors.** Include discrimination law, consumer law, anti-competition law, employment law, and health and safety law. These factors can affect how a company operates, its costs, and the demand for its products.

▶ **Environmental factors.** Include ecological and environmental aspects such as weather, climate and climate change, which may especially affect industries such as tourism, farming and insurance. Furthermore, growing awareness of the potential impacts of climate change is affecting how companies operate and the products they offer, both creating new markets and diminishing or destroying existing ones.

There are many different templates you can use for a PEST (or PESTLE) analysis but the essential questions to ask are:

▶ What things might change?

▶ Are they changes in the long term or short term?

▶ Are these changes likely to have a high, medium or low impact?

▶ Are they internal or external?

▶ What action will you take?

SWOT analysis

By looking at your company through the SWOT framework, you will be able to craft a strategy that will help you align your Strengths with market Opportunities, improve your Weaknesses, and avoid outside Threats. Not only that, but this is a great way to distinguish yourself from your competitors.

Create a grid with four sections, one for each component: Strengths, Weaknesses, Opportunities and Threats.

	Helpful to achieving your objective	Obstacles to achieving your objectives
Internal origin	Strengths	Weaknesses
External origin	Opportunities	Threats

▶ **Strengths**: Start by listing things that are helpful to achieving your objective. What does your business do well? What advantages do you have over your competition? Where have you had the most success in the past? What do you provide that your competitors do not?

▶ **Weaknesses**: Think about things within your business that are harmful to achieving your objective. What are your areas of difficulty? What are things that you could do better? What are your needs? What do your customers complain about? What do your employees (if any) complain about?

▶ **Opportunities**: This is where you list external factors that influence your company. What new technologies can you utilise? Are there local businesses or organisations that you could work with? Can you take advantage of new social patterns, lifestyle changes or cultural trends? Do you have a list of local events where you might find opportunities?

▶ **Threats:** What are some external obstacles that you face? What is your competition doing? Are there new developments threatening your business plan? Are you in debt?

The SWOT analysis is a quick and easy way to understanding the big picture and is the starting point of strategic planning. The four quadrants of the SWOT grid can also be used together. For example, look at the Opportunities you've identified and how, if you can overcome your Weaknesses and improve your Strengths, you could take advantage of them.

You can also use the SWOT method on your competitors. As you do this, your strategy will improve and you will see how and where you should be competing.

Utilise Strengths and minimise Weaknesses. Take advantage of Opportunities and avoid Threats.

The final step is the most important of all – applying the results. Utilise your Strengths and minimise your Weaknesses. Take advantage of Opportunities and avoid the Threats.

> Check your SWOT analysis with your growth plan and make any adjustments. Then stick the plan on your wall. You'll be amazed at how much it helps with decision making!

Managing risk

Wherever you are on your growth journey, risk management must be an integral part of day-to-day business activity. As your business grows, the risks you face will change and your processes for managing risk must evolve.

Are you focused on the right risks?

If you have done a PEST and SWOT analysis, you will have identified some risks. How we assess the risks determines how we act. Despite any protestations of weighing up pros and cons, we nearly always make decisions based on how we feel and not on facts.

As your business grows, investors and other stakeholders will want assurance that you understand the key risks facing your business and that you have these under control.

Familiar risks may manifest themselves in different ways; you may encounter new kinds of risk for the first time. The way your business deals with risk will need to evolve. Take a broad view of risk issues. Understand that threats can emerge from any part of your own business and from broader environmental and industry changes.

Don't limit your risk analysis to your own company. Consider how new risks could affect your complex value chain of suppliers, customers, business partners and stakeholders.

All organisations are exposed to a number of internal and external events that have the potential to disrupt the business.

> List all of the risks you think your business might need to plan for. These could include:
> ▶   losing all your data in a flood or fire or through human error or hacking
> ▶   losing key members of staff.

Go through the list and decide what you can do to mitigate the risk or how you will deal with the situation if it should arise. Strategies could include:

▶ Accept the risk that the event will occur and ignore it because the cost of treating it outweighs the benefits to be gained.

▶ Change the part of the business process that would be affected by the risk because the probability and impact are high enough to warrant intervention.

▶ Transfer the risk to another party, such as an outsourced supplier, because they are better equipped to deal with the risk.

▶ Take steps to reduce the probability and limit the impact.

▶ The objective is to maintain the required level of operation so that your business can continue to serve its customers and satisfy its obligations.

Infrastructure and systems

Most growing companies are so focused on their ability to produce now that they spend little effort on building the operational infrastructure and systems to sustain that growth over time. Think of building your business as a franchise. You want anyone to be able to pick up your operations manual and run the company just the way you do. A good tip is to streamline any manual work processes before you tinker with the technical systems. It's easy to install a new computer system but it won't reduce the risk if all you do is automate inefficiencies.

A good infrastructure can free you up to work on further developments in your business.

A good infrastructure can free you up to work on further developments in your business – or to take time off knowing that everything will get done the right way.

Good data

Good decision making relies on good data. 'Gut-feelings' usually result in slow or poor decision making and this can spell disaster. These days there are tools to measure just about anything and a corresponding risk would be to drown in data and not know what is important and what isn't. Identify and focus on the key success factors and corresponding measures, then integrate your systems to capture the data you need.

Continuity planning

When a business is growing it is smart to plan for at least the next two years. A lot of the planning process is included in Chapter One – Managing the business, but as well as general planning it is important to have a continuity plan that will satisfy investors and potential clients that you have thought about, recognised and planned for the major risks that could disrupt your business. Translate broad strategy into specific, measurable actions and review the plan often. It is crucial to do financial planning with a long time scale as raising funds usually takes a lot longer than most people anticipate. More businesses fail because they run out of money than for any other reason.

Hire the right team

This is a very common risk factor and probably the toughest one to address. Frequently, the needs of a growing business surpass the skills of the employees that helped build the business. This forces tough decisions in order to sustain the company's growth. Selecting and promoting the right people is the biggest controllable factor in sustaining your growth. Like most decision making, employee selection is fundamentally emotional. The common approach to hiring for key positions is to recruit from companies of comparable size. However, as your business grows these employees are soon in new territory along with everyone else. A better idea is to hire for key positions from bigger companies (those that have good habits!) so these employees can help drive your vision because they've been there before. There is more on this topic in Chapter Nine – Managing people.

Financing growth

To obtain any kind of growth finance you will need a very well prepared plan that sets out projections and reassures investors that you are a good risk and that they will get their money back. There is more detail on these different aspects in Chapter Three – Managing finances, but here is a quick overview of the options available:

▶ small business loans from your bank

▶ angel investors (people who invest for a share of your business)

▶ crowdfunding, or open capital.

Crowdfunding – the new option

The crowdfunding option serves two purposes: as well as raising money, it is a great way to assess market interest. If total strangers are prepared to invest in your business for very little reward it shows that there is a public desire for whatever it is you are offering. Dominick Reed took photos of himself every day for two years and, at the urging of friends and fans, raised £10,717 on Kickstarter to publish them in a book.

Luke Lang, founder of CrowdCube, raised funds through the crowd to start his crowdfunding business, showing that there is a great appetite for alternative finance.

Crowdfunding serves two purposes: as well as raising money, it's a great way to assess market interest.

Clive Rich of LawBite started an online documents and advice service that aims to offer 'a low-cost and easy-to-understand service' to the UK's 5 million small businesses. Its prospectus predicts total sales of £9.7 million and gross profit of £4.3 million by the end of 2016. In May 2013 it raised some £450,000 after pitching on CrowdCube. By the end of the formal period for investment, it had received £398,330, or 111 per cent of its target of £360,000, from 160 investors. In a second round of fundraising it raised 15 per cent of its £120,000 target on the CrowdCube website in one day. The final result was £168,690 from 181 investors for 9.11 per cent of its equity (**https://lawbite. co.uk/**).

There are many different crowdfunding platforms. Some, like CrowdCube and Seedrs that offer equity in a business, have very strict criteria; others, like Kickstarter that are for one-off projects, offer 'perks' in return for pledges of money.

The market is now so crowded that there are specialist businesses like Crowdsurfer that help people to match their project to the most appropriate crowdfunding site and advise on how to set up campaigns.

Crowdsourcing growth ideas

The crowd is not only useful for investment; it can be used to guide expansion ideas.

James Watt started his award-winning brewery in 2007 during breaks from his day job on a fishing trawler. The name BrewDog was inspired by Watt's pet dog. He started brewing craft beer and took on the big breweries because he wants to 'put flavour and integrity and passion back into people's glasses'.

From humble beginnings in a small warehouse near Aberdeen, the firm's last set of results showed an impressive £2.5 million profit on turnover of £20 million. Right from the start, Watt and his co-founder, Martin Dickie, used social networks to crowdsource ideas for new flavours of beers and to grow an army of devoted fans. The most recent product was created by their fans who picked the name and key ingredients for the beer#Mashtag on Twitter.

The firm's approach to finance has been equally idiosyncratic. Its 'Equity for Punks' fund-raising scheme offers beer lovers the chance to buy shares at £95 a pop. The company made a net profit of just £437,000 in 2012 but it has reported that its average annual growth since foundation in 2007 has been 167 per cent.

In return, investors get a 5 per cent discount in the 12 BrewDog bars, a 20 per cent discount in its online shop and an invitation to the annual meeting, 'basically just a huge party with beer' (**http://www.brewdog.com/**).

Including two previous offers, BrewDog has raised nearly £6 million from 12,500 investors, many of whom had never owned a share. Regardless of the financial aspects of the power of the crowd, there are more and more examples of businesses using the opportunities of easy access to customers to source ideas for expansion and feedback on existing products and services, all making it easier to take the guess work out of expansion plans.

Next steps

▶ Identify your main motivator for growth.

▶ Decide on the style of business you want to run.

▶ What formal structure do you need to have?

▶ Write your growth strategy.

▶ Produce a plan to finance the growth.

▶ Institute weekly reviews and forecasts to check that growth is going according to plan and to keep finances under control.

CASE STUDY
Social i Media

Anna Marsden and Anna Lawlor, co-owners and directors of Social i Media, talk to us about how they started their business to sustain their lifestyle and how they've been surprised at the rapid growth.

Anna Lawlor is an experienced NCTJ-qualified journalist with almost 15 years' experience across B2B and B2C titles. Previously, Anna was editor of FT Business's flagship investment title and has been published extensively.

Anna Marsden is a PTLLS-qualified trainer, with an ITQ in Social Media. A solid grounding in business finance and administration provided a strong infrastructure for the business.

They started Social i Media to help businesses and charities with media communications by providing content, training, consultancy and research. (The 'i' refers to 'interaction'.)

Both are members of the CIPR and HootSuite Certified Social Media Professionals.

How was the business funded at the start? The service sector we operate in doesn't require large initial outlays. We relied on personal savings to tide us over until we could draw money from the business. However, the business received commissions within a couple of weeks for a host of journalistic content from former colleagues who wanted to support our new venture. This meant the business had some modest cash flow from day one. Some of this was invested in Anna Marsden undertaking an ITQ in Social Media, which performed a double duty for the business: it provided an accreditation for her skills but also, since a prerequisite of the course is the set-up of accounts across all social media channels and the building of a website, it meant her time was spent laying the groundwork for promoting Social i Media. The business has always been in profit and turnover is on trend for 169 per cent growth year-on-year.

What prompted you to start your business? A failed attempt at immigrating to Canada! We both left well-paid, enjoyable jobs and our life in London to move to Vancouver. After an 'adult gap year' spent skiing and snowboarding we questioned what we really wanted.

Slowly, over long, long conversations – and more than a few beers, we started forming a business plan for our media communications company. The result was that we came back to the UK, where we had lots of contacts, and launched Social i Media.

At what point did you feel that your business was established? The branding process was really useful in defining our image, our tone of voice, what we wanted our company to convey and really bringing to life a business that has until then largely existed only in a hefty business plan. Finally having a finished logo, slogan and brand assets was a real turning point in feeling like we had an actual business behind us, not just a concept. That was around the six month mark, so it coincided with us having practised describing the business to friends, former colleagues, potential clients, and at networking events. The combination of visual branding, our confidence in our own brand and us starting to build our client base (largely across content and consultancy) was a pivotal moment in feeling that we were operating a viable business.

You mention a hefty business plan. How useful has this been? When the idea of starting a business came to us, the business plan was the first step in exploring whether or not we had a viable idea that would make money and sustain ourselves – both financially and intellectually. The process of planning was very useful as it made us look at the geographical area we were moving to, the demand of the market, our skills and connections and what we were missing. It focused our idea early on but what we envisioned in the actual business plan is *very* different to what our business has authentically grown into. So in this case, the process of planning was more useful than the actual plan, as we haven't looked back at it as often as we originally thought. Having said that, the guiding light of our mission (profitable and sustainable) came out of our business plan.

I think writing a business plan is an essential stage in developing a business idea, but like travelling, it's not necessarily the destination that counts, it's the journey.

What were the major challenges affecting the growth of the business? We are fortunate to have a fast-expanding client base and we are being approached with an increasing number of attractive work opportunities. This has introduced the challenge of scaling the business much more quickly than we had anticipated. Finding the time for both client work and our business-related work is a challenge. Also, identifying the tipping point for expansion is a challenge.

What other challenges did you have? Cash flow is a big challenge for a lot of small business (according to Barclays, it takes an average of 58 days for a small business's invoice to be paid). The anecdotes we were being told suggested this is just a harsh truism of running a start-up business.

How did you overcome them? We rejected this and decided to take a tougher stance: we changed our payment terms from 28 days to 14 days; we started highlighting our payment terms within emails at the completion of projects (with invoice attached); and would politely chase for payment the day the invoice became officially overdue. Quite quickly, our clients responded by ensuring our invoices were paid before our payment terms or, typically, one week late – so still much earlier than previously and certainly shorter than 58 days! Larger clients who have strict terms of payment themselves (such as making payment within 60 days) suggested we invoice early – before completing a piece of work for them – so as to ensure we would be paid during a period we are comfortable with. It seems a consistent, firm but friendly approach really pays off for making sure you get paid.

Who have you got support from? Friends, family and each other. It's important to have someone you can trust to tell you how it is! Initially we set up our own closed 'advisers' group on Facebook, linking friends and family who had specialisms in marketing, running their own business, business management etc. We still draw on these friends but in a less formal way now. What was interesting is that we didn't actually find it so useful to network with other start-up businesses; everyone has a different motivation, goal and ultimate vision for their business and there seemed to be a palpable crowd-think at work, which diminished this obvious difference and instead thrived on sharing negative or challenging stories more than positive ones.

Any business failure to learn from? Very early on in the business, we had a warm lead who approached us for an outsourced social media solution. In the consultations, we were so successful in demonstrating a business case for the integration of social media with responsive content into their marketing strategy that the board then chose to hire a full-time digital marketer instead of using our services. This was a tough but necessary lesson in guarding our intellectual property.

What is your vision for the business? Our business objective sounds pretty dry: to be profitable and sustainable and a vehicle for our lives. The first two – to be profitable and sustainable – are symbiotic and guide us in business and client-related decisions. We're never tempted to accept low-quality high-margin business opportunities because we feel this would be brand detrimental and therefore unsustainable. Equally, we don't compete on price because this quashes profit which squeezes the high-quality provision of services, which is also unsustainable. To not be profitable means the business model is unsustainable. We've found it to be a good rule of thumb for us.

Our vision – like us – is a bit different. We expect the business to be a vehicle for our lives; as a happy, civil-partnered couple without the constraints of a traditional family life, we want to take advantage of the flexibility this affords us and enjoy working from various locations by embracing new technologies. We're not looking for a work/life balance; we're aiming to interweave our personal lives and passions with our work lives and passions, to continue to enjoy the intrinsic nature of our work for as long as possible.

While we are open to the possibility of a merger or acquisition or becoming a listed company or any number of potential opportunities, to be attractive to us it would need to provide an excellent outcome for both us and our clients and retain the values our brand holds dear.

What tip would you offer someone who is making the transition from starting out to growing their business? If you suffer, your business suffers and you won't have any emotion or energy left in reserve for when tough challenges occur. (That's not to say, of course, it won't be damn hard work.) So don't think it's a badge of honour to brag about over-working or not taking a holiday for the last three years or working every weekend.

Don't be afraid to ask. Think big, be proactive and go ahead and push for the opportunities you're dying to have access to. If and when you get knock-backs (which you will – a lot!), be tenacious, but in a friendly non-aggressive way.

3

Managing finances

In this chapter you will learn:

▶ how small changes can improve your profit

▶ why cash is all important and how to control it

▶ how to keep track of regular payments like VAT, PAYE and Corporation Tax

▶ where to access more finance when you need it

▶ what to do to avoid running out of money

▶ how to find the most profitable activity in your business

▶ the discount myth

▶ your attitude to money

▶ the benefits of setting financial goals

▶ your next steps to managing your finances.

Ask any successful business owner about their most important responsibility and they'll answer 'managing finances'. As your business grows you may employ a bookkeeper, an accountant or even a financial director, but knowing how your business is doing financially is the one thing that a business owner should never let go of. You should always know the exact financial position of your business and have an accurate projection of what is coming in and going out in order to make the right decisions.

Knowing how your business is doing financially is one thing that you should never let go of.

The profit formula is simply:

Total sales − Costs (Fixed costs + Variable costs)

Costs involved in running your business

The following are some examples to highlight the differences between fixed and variable costs:

Fixed costs

These might include web hosting, rent, membership fees, salaries, equipment maintenance, broadband/internet costs, some production costs, insurance, utility bills, tool hire, storage, furniture.

> Write a list of fixed costs that apply to your business.

Variable costs

These might include marketing, PR, stock, stationery, software, labour, NI costs, tax, telephone costs, postage, travel, interest on loans, credit card bills.

> Write a list of variable costs that apply to your business.

When you set up your cash flow chart (see below), add actual costs to those that apply to your business, detailing when each item is due to be paid.

Cash is king

Profit is a financial benefit that is realised when the amount of revenue gained from a business activity exceeds the expenses, costs and taxes paid.

Revenue − Payments (Expenses + Costs + Tax) = Profit

Regardless of whether the business is a couple of kids running a lemonade stand or a publicly traded multi-national company, consistently earning profit is the usual definition of a successful business. As old as business itself is the saying that 'Turnover is vanity, profit is sanity and cash is king'.

Consistently earning profit is the usual definition of a successful business.

There is little point in creating a huge amount of turnover if there is no profit in the business.

Many businesses look as though they are making a profit on paper but the real test is how much cash they have to play with. Daily checks on cash flow and what is due in and out of the business is a key factor in making the right decisions.

Most businesses that fail do so because they run out of cash. There are no resources left to trade with so planning is a crucial part of ensuring this doesn't happen. Most businesses are not profitable from day one, so planning how much money is needed until the profits start to come in is essential. Amazon started trading in 1994 but didn't make a profit until 2003 so they needed a plan to have enough cash to pay salaries and development costs for nine years.

Even 'not-for-profit' enterprises need to make a profit. What they do with the profit may be different to other types of business, but they need profit to pay running costs and to expand.

Cash flow templates

Most bookkeeping packages have cash flow templates and there are many free examples available online and even videos on YouTube on how to construct one that is right for your business. It's important to use the one that suits both you and your business and not to overcomplicate it. The most popular is a simple excel spreadsheet.

Many successful business owners swear by daily cash flow checks, others find that weekly or even monthly are enough but you need to find the right balance for your needs.

A simple cash flow template

	Week 1	Week 2	Week 3	›Week 52
Income				
Income from sales				
VAT rebate				
Other income				
	Total	Total	Total	Total
Outgoings				
Wages				
Insurance				
Web hosting				
Supplies				
Travel				
Rent				
Interest charges				
Bank charges				
Other outgoings				
	Total	Total	Total	Total
Income – outgoings = cash available				

Regular financial tasks

More businesses stop trading through lack of cash than for any other reason. Make time for regular daily, weekly and monthly tasks as well as quarterly and annual reviews – appropriate to your business. Start by creating a check list of activities, such as in the template below. Every business will have a different checklist so it's important to make sure yours is comprehensive and suitable for your unique business situation.

Here are some examples that you can include in your template, followed by some notes on the activities.

Frequency	Task	Notes
Everyday activities	Bank cash (and cheques if anyone still uses them!)	
	Check bank balance	
	Check cash flow	What is due in and out in the next few days and weeks.
Weekly activities	Credit control[1]	This is essential to maintain cash flow.
Monthly activities	Review cash flow	Are you meeting your targets? (May be needed as a weekly activity.)
	Despatch invoices	Some businesses will do this weekly or even daily.
	Pay suppliers	
	Reconcile bank statements[2]	
	Prepare management accounts[3]	
	Breakeven calculation[4]	

(1) Credit control. First decide on your terms. Many small businesses ask for payment on receipt of invoice or at the most within 30 days. It's always advisable to have this conversation with your customers before you agree any work with them. If they insist on 60 days credit or longer then you will know: (a) whether you want to work with them; (b) when to start chasing them. Beware of large companies that say they only pay after 90 days as this can often cripple a small business. In a case like this it's worth negotiating up front, sometimes by getting an agreement to invoice at the start of the job rather than the end or to get a deposit before work starts.

Ideally, contact your customer before the agreed terms have passed to prompt them into including you in their next payment run. If an invoice remains unpaid after the due date, call weekly until it is paid, backed up by an email confirming the details of the call. Many simple accounting packages will send automatic reminders but, failing this, your cash flow chart will remind you. It's vitally important not to let payments get out of hand and a phone call will often get better results than written reminders.

(2) Bank reconciliation. A reconciliation compares what the bank has recorded compared with what you have recorded in your accounting programme. This helps to identify discrepancies and picks up things like bank charges that might not appear elsewhere.

(3) Management accounts. These can be simple calculations that show how much you are spending on a particular item, e.g. postage, or compares actual expenditure to budgets or one month against another to pick up seasonal variations or trends.

(4) Breakeven calculation. Take total income and compare to total expenses for the period. At the breakeven point, no profit has been made, nor have any losses been incurred and it is a good indicator that action must be taken to improve profits in the next month.

Accounts, VAT, Corporation Tax and PAYE

All businesses need to prepare some sort of accounts, either for legal purposes or in order to understand how the business is performing. Personal Tax and Corporation Tax can only be calculated using accounts but the accounts for each business differ dependent upon its size and the appropriate accounting and taxation regulations.

To manage any business some form of basic bookkeeping is an essential minimum requirement.

Most small companies and LLPs (Limited Liability Partnerships) do not need to file full accounts if the turnover is less than £6.5 million and they meet other balance sheet and employment criteria and most can also submit unaudited accounts. These exemptions do not, however, remove the obligation to prepare full accounts for shareholders.

To manage any business, especially through stages of growth, some form of basic bookkeeping is an essential minimum requirement.

Many business owners ruin their evenings and weekends by doing basic bookkeeping. While it is essential to know the numbers in your business it is hugely beneficial to employ a bookkeeper to present you with the figures you need. If you are doing your own bookkeeping and it isn't something you enjoy or something that comes easily to you, work out how many hours you spend on this job and how much a bookkeeper would cost you to do the same job (they'll do it in a lot less time and usually at a lot less than your time is worth). This proves that a good bookkeeper is worth every penny, especially as they will also save you a lot in the more expensive fees an accountant charges.

VAT

We may not like VAT, but we certainly can't ignore it as it applies to most goods and services, and it is now one of the main sources of income for HM Treasury. It is essential, therefore, for any person starting out in business to give some time to thinking about VAT. By now, however, your turnover may be approaching the VAT threshold that will require you to become VAT registered, if your business hasn't already. If you're unsure what the threshold is, then visit **http://www.hmrc.gov.uk/** to check as it's often updated at the annual Budget.

There is a standard rule when it comes to VAT, but with a few special schemes that are discussed below.

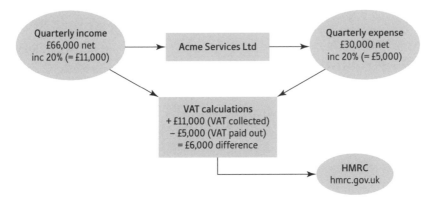

A brief VAT explanation

Let's start with the Standard VAT Scheme. Once you become VAT registered, you'll need to start adding VAT to the rateable items on your invoice. For the purpose of this exercise, let's say the current VAT rate is 20%. This means that an invoice you raise that was £6,000 has now become £7,200. This extra £1,200 belongs to HMRC, so if you haven't already by this point, open a VAT account with your bank to put money aside for the tax man.

At the end of each VAT quarter, you will need to file a VAT 100 with HMRC, which will calculate what you owe them. For example, if you've collected £66,000 of vatable income, £11,000 will belong to the tax office. However, if you've paid £30,000 in vatable supplies, then £5,000 will be money you've paid out that HMRC owe you. Once you've completed your VAT 100, it will highlight that the amount you owe will be the difference between what you've paid in VAT and what you've received – in this case, £6,000. If the VAT you paid over the VAT quarter exceeds the amount you've received, you'll then be entitled to a VAT rebate.

The VAT registration process mentions a number of special schemes. You should consider these as they are designed to help you. There will be cash flow benefits, and, in some cases, cash benefits. These are the Flat Rate Scheme, Cash Accounting Scheme and Annual Accounting Scheme.

The Single Market is now 20 years old, with many small businesses trading with the EU and beyond. The VAT rules can appear quite confusing when it comes to dealing with exports and imports, so speak to your accountant to understand all the options available to you.

PAYE

PAYE (Pay As You Earn) is only an issue if you employ people, but is still a requirement if you are a limited company and you, and/or your spouse or partner/s are the only employees. The HMRC describes PAYE as:

'... HM Revenue and Customs' (HMRC) system to collect Income Tax and National Insurance (NI) from employment. You're exempt from PAYE if none of your employees is paid £111 or more a week, gets expenses and benefits, has another job or gets a pension. However, you must keep payroll records. When paying your employees through payroll you also need to make deductions for PAYE. Payments to your employees include their salary or wages, as well as things like any tips or bonuses, or statutory sick or maternity pay. From these payments, you'll need to deduct tax and NI for most employees. Other deductions you may need to make include student loan repayments or pension contributions'.

When reporting payroll to HMRC, their website states that:

'... you'll need to report your employees' payments and deductions to HMRC on or before each payday. Your payroll software will work out how much tax and NI you owe, including an employer's NI contribution on each employee's earnings above £153 a week. You'll need to send another report to claim any reduction on what you owe HMRC (e.g. for statutory pay). You'll be able to view what you owe HMRC, based on your reports. You then have to pay them, usually every month. If you're a small employer that expects to pay less than £1,500 a month, you can arrange to pay quarterly'.

https://www.gov.uk/paye-for-employers

Real Time Information

The PAYE reporting rules known at RTI (Real Time Information) came into effect in October 2013. You absolutely must make sure your payroll process is RTI compliant as HMRC will fine those that aren't. The reason for this change is that a single Universal Credit is replacing most tax credits, a process that is due to be completed by 2017 and HMRC needs accurate information on pay and deductions to facilitate its introduction.

To ensure your payroll is RTI compliant, you need to ensure you're doing the following:

▶ Check all your employee information is accurate including name, address, date of birth, gender and NI number.

▶ Have a record of the hours that each employee regularly works in a week.

▶ Include all staff, even those under the Lower Earnings Threshold (LET).

▶ Ensure your payroll software is RTI-compliant.

▶ Send a Full Payment Submission (FPS) to HMRC as previously mentioned.

For up-to-date rules check with **http://www.hmrc.gov.uk/** or your bookkeeper.

Corporation Tax

Corporation Tax is a tax on the taxable profits of limited companies and some organisations including clubs, societies, associations, co-operatives, charities and other unincorporated bodies.

Taxable profits for Corporation Tax include:

▶ profits from taxable income such as trading profits and investment profits (except dividend income which is taxed differently)

▶ capital gains – known as 'chargeable gains' for Corporation Tax purposes.

In short, if your company or organisation is based in the UK, you'll have to pay Corporation Tax on all your taxable profits – wherever in the world those profits come from.

Surround yourself with some good advisors.

The UK tax system isn't the most complex but equally has many twists and turns. Your best bet is to surround yourself with some good advisors. Choose a bookkeeper and/or accountant who is qualified, who comes recommended and has your best interests at heart.

Key dates

For sole traders these will largely revolve around VAT, PAYE if you employ staff, and your personal self-assessment tax return. Paper returns must be submitted by 31 October in the same year following the end of the tax year in April. Online returns and any payments due must be received by 31 January in the next year.

Most partnerships will also be subject to the individual assessment of each partner's liability.

VAT returns and payments are due monthly or quarterly dependent upon which 'scheme' your business operates – most submit a return and payment quarterly but there are various options available, the most common of which is annual accounting whereby you pay monthly but only submit a return once each year. Once you are registered, these details are spelled out for you.

Incorporated businesses – those trading as a limited company – have a number of other obligations as follows:

▶ Annual Return to Companies House – depends on date of incorporation

▶ Accounts to Companies House – nine months after year end

▶ Corporation Tax payment – nine months after year end

▶ Corporation Tax Return – 12 months after year end.

Long before seeking new loans or additional investment in your business you must have control – nothing is really more important.

Expert opinion Peter Cross, Senior Manager at Haslers Tax
Consultancy and Chartered Accountants

To help us understand the next steps for the
financial implications of growing your business,
we've called in the expert. The following is from
Peter Cross, Senior Manager at Haslers Tax
Consultancy and Chartered Accountants.

'Cash is King Kong'

The biggest gorilla in the room for a business
owner is how they are going to pay their staff,
suppliers and of course, themselves. Everyone knows that the most common
cause of business failure is that the business runs out of cash. Despite this
well-known fact, small business owners often don't identify as early as possible
when cash will be low or non-existent.

Put yourself in the shoes of a bank manager. Would you rather lend money to
someone with good financial records who approaches the bank for a loan four
months before it is needed or to someone with a shoebox of receipts and a
cobbled together spreadsheet asking for credit as soon as possible?

Sounds obvious? So why do small business owners so often take the latter
approach? From my experience it is either:

▶ time pressures

▶ not knowing where to start

▶ sticking their head in the sand.

If this sounds like you, action is needed.

▶ Bring your records up to date using either a detailed and accurate
spreadsheet or dedicated software.

▶ Keep them up to date.

▶ Ask someone to nag you to keep them up to date.

▶ Prepare accurate projections for at least the next twelve months.

▶

> ▶ Revisit the projections at the end of each month and update them.

> ▶ Use your data to identify trends in your business.

'Don't be penny wise and pound foolish'

The general perception is that spending money on professional advice is an extravagance. I see a lot of businesses that have been trading for two or three years with simply awful financial systems. Bad financial systems cause huge issues including:

(a) The business owner can't plan to grow their business.

(b) It's difficult to raise finance to implement growth plans.

(c) Complying with HMRC becomes a 'near enough' exercise that can mean paying not enough or too much!

All of these are detrimental to the business and in the case of item (c) could lead to substantial fines.

Note: Anyone can call themselves an accountant so check qualifications and experience in your particular sector before engaging one and remember that a good bookkeeper can save a lot of money on accountants' fees by presenting books that are easy to turn into a set of accounts.

Access to finance

Most small businesses start with the minimum of investment, usually from the personal savings of the owner, their family and friends. In order to grow, you may need to look for other forms of investment.

Finding business finance in any economic climate can be challenging, but there are quite a few different ways to access finance and more alternative financing options to fill the gaps. The most important thing to remember is that all of these methods take time, so careful planning is essential.

1   **Bank loans**. Lending standards are tougher than they've ever been and most small businesses don't meet the strict requirements for risk-free lending that banks prefer. Interest rates are also a consideration so

check these carefully. However, most high street banks are still in the business of lending and many also have useful business services packages so it's always worth shopping around to see what's available.

2   **Crowdfunding.** Crowdfunding is a way to get small amounts of money from a lot of strangers in return for a small reward which can be in products or services or a small share of your business. There are many crowdfunding sites, all offering different deals for single, one-off ideas or projects.

3   **Angel investors.** An angel investor, business angel or informal investor is an affluent individual who provides capital for a business, usually in exchange for equity. Angel investors often organise themselves into angel groups or angel networks to spread the risk.

4   **Grants.** There are a whole raft of grants available from both national and local government and special funds set up to help specific sectors and types of business. It can be time consuming to research and there will be a lot of red tape to work through but grants often come with specialist advice so can have hidden benefits.

5   **Microloans and alternative finance.** The lack of a credit history, collateral or the inability to secure a loan through a bank doesn't mean no one will lend to you. Microloans are often so small that commercial banks can't be bothered lending the funds. Microlenders offer smaller loan sizes, usually require less documentation than banks, and often apply more flexible underwriting criteria. This is a growing sector but check terms and conditions carefully.

What is the most profitable activity in your business?

If your business is about supplying products, it is relatively easy to determine the most profitable lines. If you have a service-based business it can be trickier to figure out which are profitable activities and which are not.

Examine your business, put every activity under the microscope and be ruthlessly honest.

We all tend to gravitate to the activities that we enjoy. A photographer may love the process of taking and producing great shots but hate the idea of having to sell them. The activity of taking the pictures is essential to the business but without sales there is no business, so there needs to be a decision about how much each activity is worth and who is best suited to do them.

Pursuing high-return activities and dropping or delegating the less profitable ones is often the difference between creating profit and creating turnover. Examine your business, put every activity under the microscope and be ruthlessly honest about finding your most profitable activities and about what your time is worth.

Don't run out of cash

When you are monitoring cash flow you can spot when cash is likely to be tight. The sooner you notice this, the sooner you can do something to prevent the disaster of running out of cash.

Look at what cash came in over previous weeks and months and make informed estimates of what is likely to come in. It can help to make best, mid- and worst-case projections for what is expected.

Income – Outgoings for week, month and year = A clearer decision on what you need to do in any situation

Some of the areas you can focus on to work through cash management options include:

1 Where can you cut costs?

Look at all expenditure and consider whether it is possible to reduce each one, without adversely affecting your current quality of service. For example, buying supplies in smaller quantities may increase unit price but could help your cash flow and save you having to pay interest on overdraft or credit facilities. Savings by buying in bulk need to be balanced against how much it really costs in terms of cash flow.

Other ways to reduce costs:

▶ Automate everything that can be automated.

▶ Eliminate waste.

▶ Use cheaper materials (only where appropriate without damaging your product or service!).

▶ Pool purchases with associates – buy in bulk.

▶ Challenge price increases from suppliers.

▶ Update and change methods of working.

▶ Employ casual/part-time/contract labour.

▶ Eliminate under-performing advertising/marketing.

▶ Undertake a systematic review of all overheads.

▶ Improve negotiating skills.

2 Make paying easy

There's no better way to improve cash flow than by encouraging your customers to pay in cash or by debit or credit card or directly into your bank. Make it easy for them to pay by these options and add payment details to every invoice.

3 Turn invoices into cash

Always invoice your customers promptly and chase their payment as early as you can. Send a reminder ahead of the payment due date – it could reduce the risk of it being paid late.

You could always encourage them to pay by debit or credit card or ideally online. You could try incentivising cash upfront or early payment by offering discounts or other benefits.

4 Restructure your repayments

Talk to your bank or any other lenders you have about changing the way you repay your loans. For example, you may want to consider moving money borrowed on overdraft or credit card to a loan. This can often be cheaper and your monthly repayment costs would be more predictable.

5 Can you alter your pricing?

Look closely at what your competitors are selling. Using knowledge of your own business, estimate the cost that goes into their products or services. Using your own prices, can you estimate the level of profit in their sales? Is it more or less than yours? Is there room for you to increase your prices – and therefore your profits – and still remain competitive in your market?

6 Be prepared to buy on credit ...

... in the short term at least. If your cash flow is temporarily slowed by a problem that you're confident will be resolved soon it may be worth buying goods on credit as interest charges may be small in contrast to the profit generated through having the goods available.

7 Talk to the taxman

Before you fall behind with payments, call the tax office. You will still have to pay the amount eventually but it could make a major difference to your immediate cash position and prevention is much better than the cure.

8 Stay on top

Having worked to improve your cash flow – keep it going. Continue to forecast and regularly check your forecasts against what is actually happening to your cash levels. Daily or weekly cash flow updates can help spot problems in advance giving you the best chance to resolve them and keeping your business healthy.

Other ways to increase revenue include:

- ▶ Increase prices.
- ▶ Review entire pricing structure.
- ▶ Prune range of products/services offered.
- ▶ Weed out loss-making products/services.
- ▶ Concentrate efforts on high margin products/services.
- ▶ Invoice promptly.

▶ Get paid in advance.

▶ Don't lend customers your money (late payments).

The following are the most popular ways of increasing revenue:

▶ **Increase the number of customers**. This is the favourite avenue pursued by most business owners but is often the least effective way of increasing profit.

▶ **Increase the average order value**. Adding extra offers to regular orders can work well and is often an easier way to increase profits.

▶ **Increase the average order frequency**. Getting more sales from each customer can often be more effective as some of the costs of servicing each customer will be affected by economies of scale.

When you increase each section by just 10 per cent you end up with 33 per cent more turnover. If the profit margins stay the same or increase with economies of scale, profits will increase accordingly.

Customers	Average order value	Average order frequency	Turnover
100	£100	2x	£20,000
110	£100	2x	£22,000
110	£110	2.2x	£26,620
+10%	+10%	+10%	+33%

The discount myth

Discounting can be the death of many businesses that don't realise how badly this destroys your margins. At a profit margin of 50 per cent, if you discount your prices by 10 per cent, you need a 25 per cent increase in sales just to stand still.

Number of products sold = 100. Price = £100. Total sales = £10,000

Profit margin (10%) = £10. Total Profit £1,000

Increase prices by 10%

Let's assume 80 per cent of customers still buy from you (in reality it will probably be at least that).

Number of products sold = 80. Price = £110. Total sales = £8,800

Profit margin (now 20%) = £20. Total Profit = £1,600

So, your profit is up significantly – by 60 per cent. The numbers look dramatic because it's the difference between revenue and profit – you are adding on profit margin, which flows to your bottom line. (Remember your goal is to increase your profit – not just add sales revenue that doesn't generate profit.)

Discount prices by 5%

Get an extra 20 sales

Number of products sold = 120. Price = £95. Total sales = £11,400

Profit margin now 5% = £5. Total Profit = £600

You'd need to sell 320 products to get the same profit as selling 100 at 10 per cent margin.

Personal financial goals

There are four key figures you need to think about when you are deciding what financial rewards you want from your business:

1   What do you need to survive?

2   What will be 'OK'?

3   What will be nice?

4   What is your dream income?

It is so important to know what these figures are as these will be your markers to success. If you find that you need to tweak them as you go along, you can do that too.

1 What do you need to survive?

This is the bare minimum you need to eat, pay your bills. It's the amount that means you have enough to go on and that you don't have to go back to full-paid employment.

> Write that figure down here: . . . .

2 What will you be OK with?

This is the amount that will keep you comfortable. You can easily pay your bills, you don't have to make too many sacrifices and you're not losing sleep.

> Write that figure down here:..

3 What would be nice?

This is the figure where you're managing to have a good holiday, are able to buy some extra things for yourself and the family at the end of the month.

> Write that figure down here:..

4 What is your dream income?

What is the amount at which you know you have achieved success? You have all of the income you need to achieve the lifestyle you want to have.

> Write that figure down here:..

Now choose one of the numbers you determined above to create your financial plan. Which number you choose is up to you. However, if you are fairly new in your business or have had difficulty stabilising your income, start with one of the first two numbers and achieve that level of success first. Then as you stabilise and grow you can step into the third number and then on to the fourth!

What figure have you chosen to create your financial plan?

Your relationship with money

This is a slightly off the wall but revealing exercise!

Imagine that you have enough money to cover all your outgoings and buy the things you need and still have money in the bank. You have your dream home and it's decorated in exactly the way you want. Only one thing is missing – the perfect lamp to complete your favourite room.

Now imagine that you have found the absolute perfect lamp. You've got money – it's not going to affect your bank balance in any significant way. How much would you be prepared to pay for it?

Write down your answer.

Examine your answer and what this reveals about your attitude to money, its value and purpose in your life. If you wrote anything other than 'whatever it costs' you have set limits about value and worth.

▶ Do you see money as a tool to use to get things that you want?

▶ Do you see it as something to hang on to and to be spent sparingly in case it runs out?

▶ Do you see it as something that is easy to make more of?

When someone becomes rich they buy 'stuff', then service, then experiences. If you have 'limits' on how much you are prepared to pay for things, it may mean that even when you are rich you will deprive yourself of wonderful experiences.

Next steps

▶ If you don't already have one, create a cash flow chart.

▶ Prepare a chart of regular financial tasks.

▶ Investigate how using a bookkeeper will improve both your business and your quality of life.

▶ Find out how much a bookkeeper could save you in accountant's fees.

▶ Make a diary date of key dates for VAT, PAYE and Corporation Tax payments as appropriate.

▶ List your fixed and variable costs.

▶ Figure out the most profitable activity in your business.

Contraband International

Archie Archer has only ever worked for herself since she left University. Here, she talks about how she has grown her current business, Contraband International, over a period of ten years.

Contraband International is a corporate entertainment agency set up in 2004. It has 12 employees, turnover of £2 million and sends out approximately 6000 entertainers a year.

What prompted you to start this business?
I wanted a business that I could manage being a mum as well as working. I wanted to keep to office hours, as much as possible, and through knowing a lot of performers, I thought that maybe I could move from being a performer to being an agent.

I was so busy the minute I added all the performers to the website, I knew I needed a second member of staff and initially that member of staff came from the local job centre.

At what point did you feel that this business was established? I think I knew the minute I moved into an office. When I was a sole trader and working from home, I used to turnover £80,000 a year, which I was quite impressed with, but when I moved into an office, within five months, I got up to £250,000 with four staff, and that's where I think I had a business. With hindsight, looking back, I'm sure I felt I had a business when I was working from home, but it felt much more established once I'd moved into a permanent work space.

What has been the biggest challenge over the last ten years? There have been loads. I don't have a degree in business; I've never worked in an office so some of the biggest problems have been about assuming that when you hire a professional like a bookkeeper or an accountant that they know their stuff. When you're employing people, I think it's really important to have an understanding of what to expect so that you can check to make sure that they're doing the job right. At one point, I wasn't sure if we were technically solvent or we had gone out of business and that was a huge lesson.

Who supported you when growing your business in the early stages? In the beginning when I was first starting out, I was set up by the Prince's Trust and had a business mentor. Recently, I've put together something called the Events Gang. It's a group of seven business entrepreneurs, all working in the same industry, not conflicting with each other, and we meet once a month to be able to share information. Sometimes when you run a business, the best mentor, the best advice you can get is from another business owner and it could be from a completely different industry. The idea of the Events Gang is to share information but also for accountability.

Being an entrepreneur and running a business is a little bit like a child that's been given homework. You'll get some who will diligently do their homework when they're given it and then you're going to get others who will do their homework in the 23rd hour. The point of the group is meeting fellow business owners and talking about what they're going to be doing strategically. When you run your own business, you work for yourself. There isn't anyone else there checking on what you're doing and so it's useful to have other business owners as your support network.

What other advice would you give to a business owner making the transition from starting out to growing their business? A key lesson I was told when I was 11, from my best friend's dad, is: 'minimum effort for maximum reward' and that just means to work smart. Every single thing that you're doing should be done in the most efficient way.

Write down every single task that you have in your business from marketing to PR to sales, the accounts, everything. Obviously, when you first start and it's just you, you're doing all of it. But as you grow the business it's really good to make sure that those roles are clear and defined.

CHAPTER FOUR

Managing social media

Arguably one of the biggest disruptors in business in recent times, social networks can't be ignored. Facebook, Twitter, LinkedIn, YouTube, Pinterest, Google Plus and many, many more are now essential communication channels for many businesses.

If you are one of the business owners that think you don't need to use social networks because your customers don't use them, think again!

In this chapter we're going to explore:

▶ ways to use social media for business growth

▶ the contradictions of social media

▶ the myth of numbers

▶ establishing trust

▶ how to listen to customers, competitors and more

▶ what the most popular platforms offer

▶ how to use influencers and amplifiers

▶ the importance of great content

▶ how to measure your return on investment

▶ how hashtags work

▶ automation and timesavers.

The most popular activity for small businesses on social networks is marketing, but there are many other very useful opportunities that can be used to great effect to help grow a business.

Ways to use social media for business growth

▶ To identify and attract potential customers.

▶ To engage with existing customers.

▶ To attract, influencers and referrers.

▶ To give superb customer service.

▶ To listen to what is being said about you and your competitors.

▶ To keep up with industry trends and news.

▶ To build a community.

▶ To improve SEO.

▶ To publish links to information (articles, blog posts etc.).

▶ To promote special offers, competitions etc.

▶ To demonstrate expertise.

▶ To share values.

Most social networks accept paid-for advertising, but creating this type of ad is a job for a professional. As with any other type of advertising media, campaigns get a better return than a single ad but this usually needs a big budget!

The contradictions of social media

Social media marketing is a very different activity to traditional, 'other' media marketing. Television, radio and print are all broadcast media, used to send out information, whereas social media is most successful when people are engaged in a two-way conversation.

For all its promised benefits, including fast access to large numbers of potential customers, a recent report from Citibank reveals that 76 per cent of the 500 organisations surveyed have not found social media useful in generating business (**www.citi.com**).

This is mostly because people don't join social networks to be sold to and, while most will accept adverts as the price for a free service, they definitely don't want their conversations and games to be interrupted by sales and marketing messages. Some of the contradictions are summarised in the following table:

Nobody has ever joined a social network to be sold to	vs	Businesses are told its great place for marketing
There are millions of people on social networks	vs	Most of them only connect with people they already know
Social networks are free to use	vs	They cost business a huge amount of time and money
People go there to waste time, have fun and connect with friends	vs	Businesses keep trying to sell to them
People like to connect to businesses in a way and time that suits them	vs	Businesses prefer broadcasting to reacting to customer requests
People share a huge amount of information about themselves	vs	Most businesses aren't listening

This means that that biggest benefit to businesses is not to sell or interrupt but to listen, to react authentically and to be personal.

Success in social media isn't about mass communication

The true power in social media engagement for businesses rests in the conversations between specific people, not the masses. Focusing on the size of our online communities and the 'power of many' has proved to be a huge distraction, so much so that we've missed the true value of social media networking for businesses: The insights and power of one-to-one conversations.

The power in social media engagement is in the conversations between people.

Within a large online community, you may have many people engaged in a group conversation. Group conversations serve to highlight issues, publicly debate commonly held beliefs, or make the larger community aware of trending topics. The net result is almost always 'awareness'.

When two people within a defined relationship (such as co-workers, family members, etc.) speak to each other about a specific product (e.g. smartphones, groceries, insurance, etc.) and at a specific time in the consumer-buying cycle (awareness, consideration, decision), the result is often behaviour change.

Broad awareness is often required as part of the business's sales and marketing mix; however, any effect on gross revenue or profits is often anecdotal.

Good practice

SnoozeShade is a range of sun and sleep shades to fit baby buggies. Founder Cara Sayer says that Twitter has played a crucial role in building SnoozeShade's success: 'It's a key part of my business. Twitter provides a very active and direct way of communicating with people. I can easily connect with journalists, suppliers and customers, and I've made some really important business connections through it.' The @SnoozeShade account (with Cara's face to emphasis personal service) now has over 8,000 followers. SnoozeShade also has nearly 6,000 active Facebook fans and runs regular chat sessions, allowing customers to connect with each other as well as with Cara. Started in Surrey in 2008, SnoozeShade sold 10,000 shades in the first year, more than 20,000 in the second and it's grown each year since with outlets in many different countries all over the world. Cara does have help with her social media activity but still does most of it herself – often from her smartphone while she's on the move.

The myth of numbers

Social media godfather Gary Vaynerchuck maintains that success in social media is 10 per cent content and 90 per cent engagement and that the influence of followers is more important than the number.

For example, it would be easy to dismiss someone who makes a complaint on Twitter if they only have six followers. If one of those six followers happens to re-tweet the message to her followers and one of those people happens to be a friend who is also a reporter for a national TV news show, what happens? What if that reporter brings the story to the producers and all of a sudden it's on the six o'clock news? The absolute number just doesn't matter. You could have ten followers, or 1,000,000 followers, all it takes is for one tweet to be noticed by one person, and the word-of-mouth magic that social networks are will take care of the rest.

If numbers don't matter why do people buy fake followers and fans? Why do 'social influence' platforms like Klout, Kred and PeerIndex take numbers of followers and fans into account?

Some numbers do matter. A blog post with lots of comments, likes and/or +1s is a clear indication that people have read it and like it. A tweet that gets re-tweeted is hitting the mark. A Facebook post that gets shared on other people's timelines is having some impact.

The numbers that don't matter much on their own are Twitter followers and Facebook page 'likes'. Unfortunately, these are the ones that are most often measured as indicators of success in social media.

It's easy to get a large number of Twitter followers by using an autofollow tool. This means that when people follow you – even if they are bots (robots) or fake accounts, you automatically follow them back. You can easily spot the accounts that use these tools as the number of people they follow and the number of people who follow them will be roughly equal – often in the thousands. This means that there are millions of Twitter accounts run by bots all following each other but never talking to each other or seeing what each other says.

Brands and people for whom it is important to look popular may start a Twitter or Facebook account with lots of bought 'fake' followers or fans, hoping to replace them with real ones, but lack of interaction or good content often puts off the real people so it becomes a self-defeating cycle.

Approximately 90 per cent of people who like a Facebook page will never visit that page again or see its posts, making the effort put into the acquisition of those numbers futile and the numbers themselves meaningless.

Don't be fooled by a competitor who apparently has a lot of followers or fans. In a recent analysis of a company that has 4,000 Twitter followers 50 per cent were fake or inactive and 10 per cent non-English speaking. You can get more fans or followers by offering incentives and competitions but if the only reason someone likes your page or re-tweets your message is to win an iPad they're not much use to you, unless you can collect their data and use it in some other way.

For small businesses, it really isn't about the numbers; it's about an opportunity to connect on a personal level. It's about making people care and

The best use of social media for a small business is in putting a personal face to your business.

they're only going to care about you when you've demonstrated that you care about them.

The best use of social media for a small business is in putting a personal face to your business, listening for opportunities to be helpful and useful, being available to answer queries and best of all, figuring out who the influencers are in your sector and how you can get their attention.

Degrees of trust

Social media has taught us that we trust other people more than brand advertising and paid spokespeople. Yet, not all people are created – or trusted – equally.

There's a fundamental difference in the trust attributed to the collective voice of our social community than that given to individuals with whom we share personal experiences.

The collective voice of our community may agree that Brand X has the best car insurance but we often choose an insurance company based on the experiences of our trusted friends and family members. The point is that individuals – and their relationships with each other – generate action. That's what influences others to truly consider or purchase a product. These relationships have the power to deliver all that social media has promised to businesses.

Big businesses that get this now go to great lengths to make their communications personal; they hire and train staff to build communities and networks and to engage with customers and potential customers on a very personal basis.

Owners of small businesses are often encouraged to hide their personality behind business names and logos in the interests of creating 'brand awareness' when it has been proved that this is not what customers want and more importantly, not what works.

> ### Good practice
>
> *National Geographic* launched a contest on Facebook where fans can experience the thrill of having their own photo in a *National Geographic* magazine. Fans simply upload their photos through Facebook, caption it, and then are entered to win a travel package. Seems like a great image generator that fans will also want to share on their own Facebook pages.

Social media listening

The mass of conversation on the internet is a goldmine. Our customers and potential customers are talking to each other all the time. People we would like to notice us, to recommend us or to send us referrals are out there chatting. The good news is that we can monitor these conversations relatively easily and use them to our advantage.

The mass of conversation on the internet is a goldmine.

Imagine a customer telling a friend that they have just had a great (or bad) experience with your company and you pop up and say thank you, that's great to hear, (or sorry, how can I help to put it right?). Everyone loves that kind of attention, especially from the business owner!

There are many different ways to use social listening or monitoring so it's important to know what you want to achieve. You might want to monitor competitors as well as gather intelligence on your customers or get noticed by thought leaders in your industry.

There are many tools being developed to do this, from free Google Alerts and dashboard applications to very sophisticated and expensive software suites that integrate with Contact Relationship Management (CRM) systems.

> ### Good practice
>
> Wedding site Offbeat Bride (**offbeatbride.com**) has a wonderful Pinterest account that not only pins content from their own site, but also general wedding information and inspiration. The account is a must-follow for soon-to-be brides using Pinterest, and has a great conversion rate for sending traffic to their website.

Which platforms best suit your needs?

New platforms and networks are popping up all the time but its best to use a few really well than to spread yourself too thinly. The best rule of thumb is to go where your target audience is. When reading the information below please bear in mind that nothing changes faster than a social network!

1   **Facebook.** Take note that 90 per cent of fans who 'like' a Facebook page never return. Unless they actively comment on and share your posts, 50 per cent of fans won't see your content after three months. Posts that include pictures get a lot more traction. Facebook actively penalises text-only posts. Its use for B2B marketing is limited and it takes a lot of time and effort to get any traction. With persistence and originality it is possible to build a loyal following but the return on investment is generally very poor.

2   **Twitter.** The life of a Tweet is about six minutes. It's a real-time platform for conversations. The power of Twitter is in getting re-tweets as this extends the life and reach of your messages. To do this your tweets must be useful, funny or unusual. Pictures and links are shared extensively and Twitter is particularly good for bringing people to your blog or website.

3   **LinkedIn.** LinkedIn is the place where people go to check out your qualifications, credentials, references and experience. Publishing blog posts and taking part in group discussions that establish you as an expert and thought leader are some of the most useful activities. You can also keep track of competitors by checking new staff appointments and find new employees for your own business.

4   **Google+ (Google Plus).** Many people have a love/hate relationship with Google Plus. The jury is still out about its use for engagement but it is top for search engine optimisation (SEO) and great for free video conferencing (Hangouts) that can be published automatically to YouTube.

5   **YouTube.** Owned by Google and an even bigger search engine, YouTube is one of the biggest social networks and probably the most powerful platform of all. You can set up your own branded channel and get

people to subscribe to your videos in the same way they would subscribe to a podcast.

6 **Pinterest.** As the fastest stand-alone site ever to reach 10 million monthly unique visits, it's a beautiful and intuitive user platform. Before you dismiss it as a female/retail/craft-centric place, consider the professional services and other businesses that use it to post infographics to drive unprecedented numbers of new visitors to their websites. Check out General Electric's pin boards **http://pinterest.com/ generalelectric**. Images are the most shared medium on the web.

7 **Instagram.** One of the most popular social networks for photo sharing that the mobile web has ever seen. Many bloggers build huge followings here and fashion brands report that it drives sales.

Good practice

Shopatrend is an online site that sells women's clothing and accessories. Despite having just a small number of followers on Twitter and Facebook (less than a hundred), they have more than 6,500 followers on Instagram. They share the latest fashion trends such as clothing, accessories and women's products that generates an average of 150 likes-per-photo, driving traffic to their website where the sales are made.

---

8 **Quora.** The quality of questions asked and answers provided is extremely high. While Quora might not be the right network for your business as a major traffic driver, it could be a great place to build your company's authority and thought leadership, generating much higher quality leads in the long run.

9 **Meetup.** A true business network, Meetup makes it easy for anyone to join groups that meet face to face and to follow up and keep in touch online.

10 **Wordpress, Blogger and Tumblr.** Blogs are the original social networks, these are three of the most popular free platforms where you can discover and follow other blogs.

It's worth remembering that most people access social networks on mobile devices so make sure your content looks good on all screen sizes.

Influencers and amplifiers

There are several businesses that claim to measure people's social influence. Klout, Kred and PeerIndex among others use algorithms that measure interactions and come up with a score. Klout once famously gave Justin Bieber a higher influence score than President Obama so these need to be treated with care. Nevertheless, people get upgraded on flights and in hotels, get products to review, free perks and even job offers based on these scores. Knowing how to work the system means that people can 'game' it, acquiring a higher score by adopting certain behaviour. For most small businesses they're best ignored. Go with who you know to be influential irrespective of their activity on social networks.

Go with who you know to be influential irrespective of their activity on social networks.

A social media presence can multiply influence to a huge degree but can also create other influencers outside of the celebrity circus.

Influencers may give you the key to the type of content that works best in your sector. If they speak on specific topics it could allow you to gain a greater understanding of those topics and produce your own content with your own views.

When you produce content you will naturally post it on your website, blog, Google Plus page, YouTube channel etc. However, it is important to place content in places where your customers are most likely to see it and by observing where the key influencers place their content you could get valuable clues about where to post yours.

If you choose to engage with an influencer directly you need to understand what they are currently writing and talking about, what their interests are and, over time, build a relationship such that the influencer may choose to review your product or service which could lead to some excellent publicity and exposure.

Good practice

The management at the Roger Smith Hotel, a small boutique hotel, knew they had to find a way to stand out from the rest of the industry, so they turned to Twitter. To get started, hotel management did what a lot of businesses do: they had a lunch party, but instead of simply inviting journalists and local dignitaries they invited social media influencers to try out their services. As those influencers took to Twitter to share their experiences, the Roger Smith Hotel got its brand in front of a much larger audience.

The hotel didn't stop there. The team took that boost and ran with it. Now their Twitter feed is lively with trivia, coupons, pictures and more. They even give discounts to customers who reserve a room via Twitter and the hotel has a Twitter kiosk in the lobby!

Using this information, start to think of the influencers in your market and the routes you can use to reach them. This could include both online and offline activity, from traditional press releases, events with VIP guests, samples of products to review, interviews and seeking their opinion to reading and commenting on their blog, engaging them in conversation on Twitter, liking and sharing their Facebook or Google Plus posts and engaging in discussions with them on LinkedIn.

Amplifiers are people in your network who admire your work and are happy to share your content with their own audience, 'amplifying' it to a greater number of people.

Produce content worth sharing

One of the things busy business owners worry about regarding social media is how to create engaging content. There are people who advocate a content calendar and strive to produce relevant content on a regular basis on specific days of the week, taking into account links to public holidays or national/international events. (This doesn't mean that every business should have a lame 'Hallowe'en Special Offer'!)

A completely different point of view is that you should only publish when you have something worth saying. If you are new to creating and publishing content it may be better to have the discipline of doing something every week and before you start get at least four weeks in the pipeline and try to stay that way, bearing in mind that you will sometimes want to be spontaneous and react to events.

The ultimate aim of any piece of content is to be shared. It's about adding value. It's not a press release about your latest staff member or product, it's about sharing useful information that people will be glad to know about.

To get a tweet re-tweeted or a post shared it has to have useful information in the tweet or the post, not just in the link. Many people will see the posts on their mobiles but won't click the links. If the post promises good information they are more likely to come back to it later and share it with their own fans or followers.

A cue for producing great content is to use feedback and queries you get from your customers or the conversations that are going on about hot topics in your industry or sector. A restaurant can gather fans by publishing reviews and testimonials. If the fans have no way to communicate with each other or no reason to keep promoting the restaurant that's as far as it will go. A restaurant that sets up a way for fans to discuss their experiences, share their photos, swap recipes and wine suggestions and arrange meetings will create a community or tribe.

A cue for producing great content is to use feedback and queries you get from your customers.

Good practice

Five young men left home to go to different universities, but only one of them could cook. He started making short 'how to' videos for his friends and they shared them with their friends. By the time they left university they had a business. With over 900,000 subscribers to their YouTube channel and several million views a month, Sorted Food makes enough money from sponsored adverts to keep them all very happy.

The ROI of social media (return on investment)

Measuring the ROI on any business activity is crucial. In its simplest terms it is the figure you gain, say in increased sales, minus the cost of acquiring those sales. To be of real use it should have a financial value. This may mean that you have to put a value on your time and this is no bad thing. Social networking activities can become a huge drain on time and other resources so starting off by knowing how much you will invest is a big advantage and keeps everything in perspective. Don't let anyone tell you that you can't measure the ROI of social media activities. If you can't measure it, don't do it.

How to measure ROI

▶ What monetary value do you put on your time per hour?

▶ What does it cost to get a new customer by other means (advertising, cold calling, leaflet drops etc.)?

▶ How much is one sale worth (turnover and profit)?

▶ What is the lifetime value of a customer (how many times do they buy)?

Value of sales gained £1,000

Less time and money invested £750

= Return on investment £250

Hashtags#

One of the most useful ways to manage social media content is by learning how to use hashtags. A hashtag is a word or phrase with no spaces or punctuation marks prefixed with the symbol # and used on Facebook, Twitter, Google Plus, Pinterest and Instagram, among others.

Hashtags provide a way to search for messages containing the same word or groups of words but is only connected to a specific network and can't be linked or connected to pictures or messages on different platforms. A Google search for a specific hashtag will bring up posts on Google Plus but not on any other network.

Some hashtagged words or phrases are just for fun (e.g. #justsayin, #gladitsfriday, #cookiemonster, #facepalm, #wineoclock) and used as a sort of shorthand for a joke.

Others are blatant (and largely useless) marketing tags from people selling their services (e.g. #hr, #coaching, #mentoring, #bookkeeping). Since these words can be searched for without the hashtag it just looks lame and is likely to put people off reading your messages.

Using more than two hashtags in a sentence (e.g. 'These #cookies from #JanesCookieShop are #mouthwatering and #delicious #nomnomnom') is likely to get you #unfollowed #pbq!

The most useful way to use a hashtagged word or phrase is for a specific event. Conference organisers use them to great effect to help attendees connect before and after an event and to track who is talking about it. There are specific tools that enable the reach of hashtags to be tracked.

They can be used for physical events and virtual ones like Twitter chats (e.g.#designerhour).

Hashtags are a useful search tool and connector but use sparingly!

Good practice

#SmallBizSatUK is an ongoing campaign that started in 2013. An impressive 48 per cent of consumers were aware of the day with over 1.5 million Facebook views and #SmallBizSatUK trending top three all day. An estimated £460 million was spent in small businesses on the day (**https:// smallbusinesssaturdayuk.com**).

Network with purpose

More and more business networks are popping up but there is a quiet revolution going on in the way they are working. People who tweet from conferences or exhibitions connect with the speakers and each other on LinkedIn and carry on the discussion and share pictures and slides from the presentations with people who can't be there.

There is a quiet revolution going on in the way business networks are working.

These people all have a common interest, established immediately. No one does an elevator pitch and no one swaps business cards or asks for referrals. The connections will strengthen or fade according to the individual's preferences, needs and interests. Some organise casual tweet-ups, Link-ups or Google Hangouts, some have regular meetings with little or no ritual and they all offer online connections as well as face-to-face meetings at little or no cost.

Automation and timesavers

One of the biggest drawbacks for small businesses is the time they need to invest in using social networks and it can be tempting to try automated solutions or outsourcing. There are many ways to do this and most of them will alienate rather than attract your audience.

It is not a good idea to link accounts so that you post the same content to several platforms at once. However, it is possible to schedule posts to go out at different times of the day.

Hootsuite is a dashboard-style platform that enables you to view and schedule Twitter, Facebook, LinkedIn and other social networks on one screen and Buffer also enables posts to be scheduled and shared on different networks.

Scheduling allows you to reach different time zones or to space out posts but if you're not there to respond the effect is minimised. When you are more interested in having conversations than just pushing out information it becomes less of an issue.

If you haven't got the expertise to get results in house, it's best to invest in some training – bespoke for your business. Most reputable companies that offer social media services will offer training and will discourage you from getting someone else to post on your behalf. It is much better to train a skilled, experienced, trusted, valued member of staff. Never entrust your social media activities to an intern, a lowly paid employee, someone who doesn't understand the values of you and your business, someone who can't write good English or be trusted to work without a script. Always make sure YOU have the passwords for ALL of your accounts. Once the genie is out of the bottle it can't be put back in.

Next steps

▶ What is your main purpose for using social media?

▶ Research influencers and thought leaders in your industry.

▶ What sort of content will you share?

▶ Produce a content calendar for each network you have an account with.

▶ How will you measure the ROI of your social media activity?

▶ What relevant hashtags could you use (and use them to search for information)?

▶ Start to use social networks for business networking.

▶ Investigate automation and time savers.

▶ Experiment with listening tools.

▶ Which platforms do your customers use?

The Nutty Tarts

Nutty Tarts.
Gifts & Goodies

Nutty Tarts Ltd was started in 2009 by great friends Rachel and Deborah who spotted a gap in the market for cakes and biscuits that could be sent as gifts through the post.

As well as posting items direct to consumers, the company has a distribution process in place and supplies universities, coffee shops and food supply companies including 23 Waitrose outlets, as well as Andaz Hotel in Liverpool Street, London. At the time of talking to us they both still work hands on in the business and employ six members of staff.

Managing Director, Deborah Armiger, talked to us about the way the company has grown:

How was the business funded at the start? We used our own funding to begin with and business angels more recently. We didn't actually set out to use business angels but they approached us after hearing our interview on 'The Jeremy Vine Show' on Radio 2! They were interested in investing in new small businesses so we had a meeting and found a common interest so went ahead. They have a third of the business so we didn't have to sell our souls. They have been invaluable to us in terms of growing the business, both in terms of financial support and also business acumen. Having never run a business before, both Rachel and I were a bit green so it was wonderful to have someone help us through some of the hurdles we faced, particularly dealing with supermarkets. We are still involved with them five years on and consider them personal friends.

What prompted you to start your business? Having had my second child I decided that child care was too expensive for me to go back to work, so I looked at starting a business from home so that I could work around the family. I had previously done a catering Diploma and had a great passion for cake baking so decided to start an online cake business which required few overheads.

I did have a good few years working as an IT trainer so this helped greatly with setting up our website and subsequent IT requirements in the office! My business partner Rachel's background was in customer service, but she is also a very keen cook so her expertise has helped greatly with product development and scaling up our recipes to a commercial level. Our sons were in the same reception class at school so we got talking and decided to set the business up.

At what point did you feel that your business was established? Probably when we got the Waitrose deal to supply 23 regional stores, five years ago. We were invited to pitch to the Waitrose Local Buyer, John Vine, via the regional food group Tastes of Anglia which we had recently joined as a producer member, as there was a lack of quality regional cake suppliers in East Anglia so that very much worked in our favour. At the time we were still baking from home so this was a great incentive to get our business onto a more commercial footing. Our products spoke for themselves, so luckily the buyer didn't take a lot of convincing! We supply many farm shops and delis via Elveden Foods Ltd and this has worked really well for the last five years, but we are constantly looking for new outlets for our products as we'd like to expand distribution to nationwide.

If you hadn't got the Waitrose contract so early, do you think you would have stuck to your original idea of an online business and if so, what effect do you think that would have had on your growth and profitability? We would definitely have continued with the online route but it's difficult to say if we would have achieved the same success if we'd done that. We would possibly have put more into marketing the website so that might have had an effect on our growth but who knows?

What have been your most successful marketing tactics? Our company name has gone a long way to getting us lots of attention! We've managed to get some good press on the back of it – 'The Jeremy Vine Show' on Radio 2, Virgin Media's 'Small Business of the Week', *Woman* magazine, *The Sun* and various local press features. We don't have a huge budget for marketing, so rely on social media, i.e. Twitter, to help us. We also try to attend trade fairs at least once a year so that we are more visible to buyers who might otherwise not come across us.

Re Twitter: what made you decide on this platform rather than Facebook which is preferred by many B2C brands? With Facebook, if you decide to have a business page you have to commit to keeping it up to date with lots of content and that's time we don't have as a small business. Twitter is great because you can dip in and out and feed off current news and stories to keep your profile alive. You can also schedule Tweets – I sometimes sit down first thing in the morning and set up tweets to be sent throughout the day depending on what we are making/doing. We've never actually officially measured the effect of Twitter, but we've picked up followers we wouldn't normally have reached, and had the odd celebrity retweet us.

What do you recommend as the key thing to keeping customers and getting word-of-mouth recommendations? Any service provider will tell you it is customer service and a quality product that keeps customers coming back. We don't always get things right, so it's crucial we deal with things when they go wrong in a timely manner. It's human nature to tell everyone when things go wrong, and Twitter can be the downfall of many a company, so it's important to us to make sure the customer is happy and that usually means they tell their friends and family. Making sure our products are the best they can be is another way of getting recommendations – this almost does the PR for us!

Do you use any 'listening' tools or alerts so that you know if someone is talking about your brand online and you get to intervene quickly? We use Google Alerts to keep track of anything mentioning us, which has been pretty effective so far.

What is the balance of sales between supplying retail and individual online orders and which is more profitable? We are currently supplying more retail than online orders as like a lot of small businesses we don't have a very big marketing budget so rely on a combination of a small Google Adwords campaign, newsletters, packaging and local PR to drive traffic to our website. It's definitely more profitable to supply directly to the customer but we are constantly having to redevelop our products so that they sit with current demand.

What were the major challenges affecting the growth of the business? Attracting the right staff to help our business to grow, and getting the message across to buyers that quality is everything, but that it does come at a price.

How did you cope with having to manage the business instead of working in it? We are still quite small so although I manage it on a day-to-day basis, I do still have to get my hands dirty from time to time. I really enjoy this though; otherwise it's easy to lose touch with staff and what they are thinking. Rachel oversees the day-to-day production so I know things are in safe hands.

What other challenges did you have? Improving the shelf life of our products without adding nasty chemicals, and having to go through technical accreditation for Waitrose. We constantly have to 'tweak' recipes depending on the weather to get the best possible shelf life from something that only contains store cupboard ingredients, so this is always a challenge. The technical audit was a big learning curve – even though we were physically carrying out all the correct procedures, we had to make sure we developed the written evidence of this so a lot of writing/ form designing was involved!

Who have you got support from? Our families and our very wonderful business angels who have been amazing.

Any business failure to learn from? Go with your instinct – we ignored ours quite recently and it has cost us a lot of money as the project didn't work out.

What is your vision for the business? This changes constantly! Ideally we'd like to grow the business to such a level that we could look at selling it, but who knows?

Do you have any plans to open your own retail outlets? Not currently, although it is my dream to have a little Nutty Tarts van making deliveries!

What is the most useful piece of advice you had when you started? If you believe in your product, and work hard, you will succeed.

What tip would you offer someone who is making the transition from starting out to growing their business? Thoroughly test your market before making any commitments – you might think you have a great product/business idea but others might not. You do have to take some risks in business but they should be educated ones!

5

Managing technology

The world is evolving at a far faster pace than ever before and rapid advancements in technology allow us to take radical leaps forward in the blink of an eye, or the click of a mouse. The availability of cheap technology has itself generated many new types of business and even the most traditional businesses need technology to operate.

Failing to manage new technology in your business can be a huge threat.

Anyone with few insights into this world could be forgiven for feeling bewildered, but failing to manage technology in your business can be a huge threat, and while it is not as bad as failing to manage your money, there is little forgiveness or understanding for people who don't make the effort.

In this chapter we'll look at:

▶ hardware

▶ cloud computing

▶ software

▶ integrated communication systems

▶ security

▶ back-ups.

It used to be that the minimum hardware technology requirements for running a business were a computer and a phone. Now these are combined in a smartphone and tablets. Some software is designed to run only on mobile devices and, increasingly, software is developed and tested on mobile devices before being developed for desktop and laptop machines.

Hardware

Whatever requirements your business has, the standard wisdom when it comes to hardware is to buy the best you can afford and to find a reliable IT support company to maintain it and to ensure your business continuity by preventing problems rather than waiting to fix them in a crisis situation.

Taking out maintenance contracts means that your machines and devices get serviced regularly which can be extremely cost effective. There are remote monitoring programs that allow your IT support to spot potential problems, and even fix them remotely before you are aware of them, so saving a lot of time and expense.

Regularly replacing older machines with new ones gives increased speed and reliability and can vastly improve productivity.

Cloud computing

Instead of having to buy and install a server to store all of the data and programs your business needs to operate, many businesses are moving 'to the cloud'. This is the practice of using a network of remote servers hosted on the internet to store, manage and process data, rather than a local server or a personal computer. It has further transformed the way businesses work and in many cases has dramatically reduced the cost of many services.

'The cloud' has transformed the way businesses work and has dramatically reduced costs.

'The cloud' is essentially a metaphor for the internet. Marketers use the phrase 'in the cloud' to refer to software, platforms and infrastructure that are sold 'as a service', i.e. remotely through the internet. Typically, companies like Google, Amazon, IBM, Oracle Cloud, Rackspace, Salesforce, Zoho and Microsoft Azure, some well-known cloud vendors, have huge energy-consuming servers that host products and services from a remote location and they hire out the space (many also offer free services). This means that anyone buying cloud services can simply log on to the network without installing anything on their own computer. The major models of cloud computing service are known as software as a service (SaaS). These cloud services may be offered in a public, private or hybrid network.

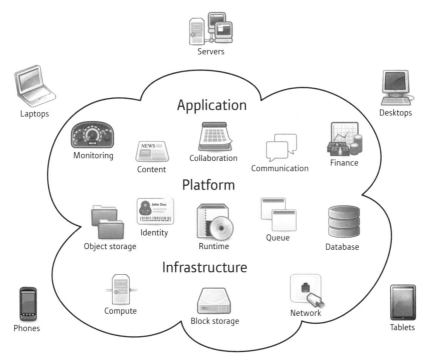

Cloud computing

Software

Everything a business needs, from diary management and bookkeeping to full-scale project management and collaborative tools is available as software applications. With traditional software applications you purchase the software upfront as a package and then install it onto your computer. The software's licence may limit the number of users (sometimes called 'seats') and/or devices where the software can be used.

Software as a Service (SaaS) allows you to subscribe to the software rather than purchase it, usually on a monthly basis. Many have free versions or free trial periods and upgrades can be purchased if needed. They are used online with files saved in the cloud rather than on individual computers.

There are a number of reasons why SaaS is beneficial:

▶ **No additional hardware costs.** The processing power required to run the applications is supplied by the cloud provider.

▶ **No initial setup costs.** Applications are ready to use as soon as you subscribe.

▶ **Pay for what you use.** If a piece of software is only needed for a limited period then it is only paid for over that period and subscriptions can usually be halted at any time.

▶ **Usage is scalable.** If you decide you need more storage or additional services, for example, then you can access these on demand without needing to install new software or hardware.

▶ **Updates are automated.** Whenever there is an update it is available online to existing customers, often free of charge. No new software will be required as it often is with other types of applications and the updates will usually be deployed automatically by the cloud provider.

▶ **Cross device compatibility.** SaaS applications can be accessed via any internet-enabled device, which makes it ideal for those who use a number of different devices, such as internet-enabled phones and tablets, and those who don't always use the same computer.

▶ **Accessible from any location.** Rather than being restricted to installations on individual computers, an application can be accessed from anywhere with an internet-enabled device.

Whatever your business need, there will be a piece of software to help you to do it online. The best piece of advice we've heard about using software as a service is 'get your human processes working well first'.

Expert opinion Yiannis Pelekanos, IDN Digital Visual Communications

Five powerful ways to use the cloud for business

The cloud has been around in public knowledge for over five years, yet many businesses are still slow to use cloud storage and computing to their full potential. The cloud can provide solutions to age-old business issues, such as difficulties with increases in scale, to decentralising work, or allowing staff to work remotely.

1 Reduce the need for disaster recovery

Handing over responsibility for storage of data, and all the issues which come with it, is arguably still the strongest reason for cloud storage. With cloud storage solutions such as Google Drive, OneDrive or Amazon S3, data is distributed locally and globally, ensuring a high level of redundancy and effectively eliminating the risk of data lost. (Redundancy is a system design in which a component is duplicated so if it fails there will be a back-up.)

2 Reduced cost

A large percentage of cloud storage and computer services run with a pay-what-you-use model meaning that you only need to buy the package that suits your storage or processing needs. Not only does this reduce cost and prevent maintenance on unused infrastructure, it also gives luxuries of scale, without initial investment.

Let's say you're a small-sized digital marketing business with multiple clients, one of which is going to have a long HD video produced and hosted. Rather than purchasing local storage for production back-ups that will have purchasing and upkeep costs, you can scale your cloud storage to accommodate for this short-term increase.

A similar policy can be taken for bandwidth requirements; if this video is placed online and goes viral, this rapid spike in traffic would have been unmanageable in the past, but with scalable hosting or cloud video services such as YouTube, this time and monetary expense disappears.

3 No need for onsite management

It's easy to think of the cloud as just software, though many of the true savings of the cloud come from its utilisation of external hardware. Cloud services take advantage of distributed servers which, when combined, form a network comprised of (often) massive data centres, in multiple international locations. Multiple data centres around Europe and the world, not only ensure a quality connection regardless of location, but are also a built-in redundancy when issues do occur.

The real advantage of this for business is massive reduction in cost that comes with fewer onsite staff and a more streamlined process. Cloud storage

▶

and computing services almost entirely remove the need for onsite system administrators and server managers.

The reality of being completely device and location independent is coming to fruition. With cloud productivity software such as Office365 combined with mail and calendar services, it is possible to work from anywhere. Remote working with 'the cloud' can mean so much more than just accessing Word, or answering emails. There are many tools that allow remote teams to come together as if you were in the same room.

4 Globalised working and increased collaboration

With the ability to work from any location, you start to have luxuries that were not available when the entire team had to be in the same room. Business meetings can now happen on the train from a tablet, just as easily as they can in front of an interactive display in a boardroom. Files can be worked on independent of device, in multiple locations, updating in real-time.

We're rapidly moving into a world where expertise matters more than location of hardware and video conferencing and remote working are big parts of that.

5 Pre-built tools and services

In the past, before the democratisation of the internet, every company had to build their own software tools. This meant that slight alterations became very expensive and many companies used out-of-date and unfit for purpose software for years. Now, due to a great deal of competition in cloud services, prices are at a race to the bottom whilst service and product have never been stronger.

Take my daily work tasks for example:

- ▶ Email – Google Apps (Cloud Mail)
- ▶ Task Management – ToDoist (Cloud Storage and Management)
- ▶ Documents – Office 365 (Cloud Productivity)
- ▶ Store Files – Dropbox (Cloud Storage)

… and that's all open before my first sip of morning coffee.

Communication systems

Customers increasingly expect to be able to contact businesses 24/7 and with many employees now being supplied with company mobile phones and tablets it can result in a confusing situation where messages are sent and received by email, landline, fax, mobile phone, voicemail, text, instant messaging and social networks.

Many businesses are choosing integrated phone systems to control the flow of information. VoIP (Voice over Internet Protocol) has the advantage of allowing customers and suppliers to be in touch with the right people without having many different numbers or calls having to be re-directed, which can mean using several phone lines or a switchboard. VoIP controls everything through the company computer and can be used for a business with several branches or for team members who work from home or who are out on the road.

In a growing business, sharing information becomes more important and VoIP allows colleagues to log in and talk to each other and see what messages have been received. For example, if a supplier has called to say a delivery is going to be late, a sales rep could pick that up and relay it to a customer without someone having to remember to send a message.

Customers really appreciate the flexibility of interacting with an organisation that can handle feedback from a range of different sources, and are even more inclined to do business with those who can offer an integrated response.

VoIP is not only more efficient but because fewer landlines are needed is also cheaper. However, it must be installed by trusted and experienced experts to avoid compromising broadband speed.

Security

Security has always been, and probably always will be, the biggest issue of using technology and the internet. Your computer could be running really slowly under the load of trojans, bots, rootkits and other malware without you even being aware of it.

Security is the biggest issue when using technology and the internet.

Whether done from criminal intent or mischief, hackers, bugs and viruses pose big challenges and can result in the loss or misappropriation of essential data.

Virus protection comes as standard with many computers now, but the free versions only protect from a fraction of the threats and are only updated every week or so whereas the more sophisticated, paid-for versions catch many more of the attacks and are updated several times a day.

It's worth paying a few pounds to get the added protection. Malware can hack into your files and access your customers' details. Not only is this embarrassing it could result in you incurring a heavy fine under the Data Protection Act.

Bring your own device

You may have company computers, laptops, tablets and mobile phones that you issue to employees but increasing, and an indication of our 'always on' world, is the trend for employees to bring their own devices to work (BYOD). This raises lots of issues about ownership of data, security, passwords and more. It's a good idea to have guidelines on how to approach this and it may be an issue you need to address in contracts of employment or your company handbook.

Always have a back-up

Data loss is bad for business. Apart from the inconvenience, failing to protect customers' data can result in hefty fines. It is estimated that 25 per cent of all computers fail in any given year and it costs a lot of money to have their data recovered. If you lose data for more than ten days your business has a 93 per cent chance of failing completely, so this is a really important issue but one that a lot of small businesses ignore.

There are a number of ways to create back-up files, but whatever method you choose, it's important to make regular checks that the back-ups are working. Too many people only find that there are flaws in their system when they try to use the back-up files. Online automatic back-up of data means that no one has to remember to do it. The other important thing is to make sure that back-ups are kept in a different location to the original data. A fire or flood that destroys your computer will also destroy your back-up files if they're in the same building.

Backing-up to hard drives

External USB hard drives come in many shapes and sizes, from larger models that often require a mains power source, to lighter, more portable drives that take their power from the USB port on your computer.

Hard drives can work out as one of the cheapest choices for backing up your data, and unsurprisingly, they're a popular choice. With your files backed-up to an external hard drive, you can carry them with you, and you'll have a valuable back-up in case your computer is stolen or damaged.

Backing-up to cloud storage

With cloud storage, all of your valuable data is uploaded to a storage provider's servers over the internet, meaning that your data is stored remotely. It's important to look at storage allowance, how long it takes to upload files, and whether there are any security risks.

Using DVDs or flash drives

DVDs are a cheap method of backing up data, while flash drives, such as USB sticks, are extremely portable.

Expert opinion Dan Frost

Dan Frost is the Technical Director of Third Eye Vision, a web and app development agency based in Hove, with clients all around the world. Dan has been co-running the business for ten years and has taken it from four to 12 people.

We asked Dan how a growing company can use technology to help them in the next

phase of their business: Choosing technology divides into what you need to catch up and what will push you further ahead of the competition. If you need to catch up you can just copy what your competition uses. When you've caught up, you can look at what will get you further ahead. It might be that no one in your field uses a CRM – contact relationship management – system. This is not unusual. There are a huge number of businesses that don't organise their data properly; this means that they can't organise follow-ups and you can't build a relationship with customers because the relationship takes time and it's a big expensive thing to do.

If you're at a certain size, say four to six people, whatever technology you're using, it becomes sticky. Once something is in day-to-day use, it's a big deal to change it; it's a long cycle, especially if your clients are using it. Suppose you have a CRM and your clients log in to the friendly side of it to access their invoices or to post questions to you. They've put a lot of investment into understanding that and as far as they're concerned that technology that they see is YOU. That's part of their experience of you as a company. So having that there means that you've got a lot of decisions made for you but you do have to be sniffing around to see what is coming next.

If someone is looking for a CRM tool what would be the core features?
The first thing to decide about choosing technology is: is this to make your day-to-day management of the company easier or is it something you want to be part of your big business processes? The first is just, 'I need Post-it notes because I can't remember all these things'. The other might be, 'I need a big task management system because I need to co-ordinate lots of people'.

If you are small and scaling rapidly and in ways you're not sure about because it's all based on demand from customers as they come in and you're learning about what it is these people want from you, I wouldn't invest tons of time in trying everything out. Find one that does just about enough.

If it's a CRM make sure you can get your data out and then you can change when you need to. If you're co-ordinating a team then the thing to start from is to get a feel for what the systems do but then go through how you want the people involved to interact. If you want to make something really scalable or just to reduce your involvement with stuff, it's nice for people to find it obvious how they're going to talk to each other. We've got an issue tracker, as many companies do. We've gone through three or four of those, and the point that it absolutely clicked was when we got a few key people in the team in a room and we walked through what the work flow should be from client to issue resolved and once you've got a flow that makes sense then everybody understands it and the client understands it and that's the thing to do. Choose a system and the way you're going to set it up based on everybody who is involved understanding it, otherwise the technology gets in the way and people get fed up with it and it just becomes a big pain.

There is such a big choice, what are the risks of choosing the wrong system and how do you avoid them? Most things have demo videos so check them out and then decide to try a few on a trial basis. Set them up as though it's a proper project, pretend to be a client and set up temporary email addresses in hotmail or Gmail and go through the whole work flow so you're really sure this will work for everyone and that you can communicate it to someone else. Once you've done that with a pretend project and you're sure it will work and you've invoiced yourself, or whatever, then you'll feel like it's going to work for you.

The thing NOT to do is to choose something because it appeared on Google ad words and it looked cuddly and friendly with not too much to learn.

When you're growing a business, what are the other key tools that a business needs? It depends on the type of business but the ones to get out of the way are the back office ones. All the finance and admin stuff. There are so many tools that will do invoicing and chase up late payments automatically. It takes hours off chasing people and is great for your cash flow.

If you're billing by the hour put a time tracker on everyone's laptop or wherever and have them put it straight in there so that you don't have to add it up at the end of the month. The other nice thing about using this type of process is that clients get used to it and the system sends the invoice and you don't have to be the person to do it.

Get all this back office stuff in place as soon as you've sent two or three invoices.

▶

You'll probably need a project management system but that needs to be approached with caution. If you're growing or you're a very small team, go as light on project management as possible until you spot a pattern in your projects. The thing I wouldn't advocate is going for something big and complicated. Go for something more agile. Keep it light and then the nice thing about that is that the project is out of people's emails and into a system and that means that you can step back and get someone else to take over the project. There's lots of choice so ask around and get opinions from people with similar sized businesses to yours.

Many businesses need a ticketing system or enquiry system for keeping track and there are dozens of those. Just Google help desk or ticketing system or issue tracker and you'll find lots. Chances are if you've ever contacted a company for help with a product it will go straight to this type of system so you can evaluate them from a customer's perspective.

Almost every business will have some kind of web presence, and some kind of content management system. As with project management, keep this as light as possible to start with. A lot of people will go straight for Wordpress but there's other free options that are sufficiently good to tell people about you and have pictures of what you do, just enough so that you can worry about getting customers and completing projects.

Like project management, as the pattern emerges, you'll understand more about what your clients are like and what they expect of your website. You'll hit a point where off-the-shelf packages are not enough.

After that you get into very specific stuff depending on what you're trying to sell. That's the point at which I'd start talking to other agencies because they will have seen more cases than you're going to have time to see and that's where you can get specialist knowledge of where you can get ahead of other people.

Next steps

▶ Looking back at your SWOT analysis, what does this throw up for your technology requirements?

▶ As Dan Frost suggested in this chapter, set up alternative email addresses and try out software applications that you think are right for you, as if you are a client. What impact does that have on your expectations? Do the applications support your internal functions or require bigger changes?

▶ Who else will be using the hardware and/or software that you choose for the business and how could this impact on the choices you make?

▶ Ask your peers what IT equipment, applications and support companies they use and what they like and dislike about them.

▶ Given its importance, do you have a reliable IT Support company that understands your business and is more interested in preventing problems than fixing them?

Clarity Heating

'To bring light where there was dark, make people warm when they have been cold and get their water running when they have had none!'

This is the purpose of Clarity Heating – a name that was chosen to reflect the philosophy and beliefs of Amelia and Mark Murfitt and Vince Rudgewick, the directors of their electrical, heating and plumbing company.

The three directors pride themselves on the way they run their business, providing a service that ensures the highest standard of work and installing the most reliable and quality products that are designed to make cost savings and fuel efficiencies for their customers. Amelia, Mark and Vince have recently taken the decision to push for high growth and intend to double their turnover and profit in the next two years.

We talked to them about how they got to this point:

How did you start? Two of us were working within the new build sector as a heating engineer and an electrician. It became apparent very early on that, in the eyes of the building companies, quality of workmanship and materials was not exactly high on the list of priorities. It was very frustrating and we knew we could offer so much more at a far higher standard without any real additional cost. That was when the idea of Clarity was born. We knew that we could do everything better. We could offer a better customer experience, give them more of the right information and offer them the right products that would enable them to make the right decision. Their choice affects their energy usage and comfort for the next 25 years so we feel it's a very important decision to make and people need the right information to make informed choices.

How long did it take from the original idea to actually running your own independent business? It actually took about two years. We knew what we wanted to do but it was difficult to make the transition from being in your comfort zone, working and getting paid, to a whole new world of uncertainty.

We eventually started in 2009 with a turnover of around £160,000. This was at the beginning of a worldwide recession. Five years later we are projecting a turnover of around £500,000 with a growth plan to break £1m in two years. We feel this is a great achievement.

How was the business funded at the start? To begin with it was just our own savings and a case of do the work, get the money in. There were lots of frustrations because while you're working onsite, doing installations, there is no one to do the invoicing and estimates so we had a real feast or famine situation going on and no real consistency. Later on we had some help from a small, private investor but mostly it was a case of generating enough revenue to invest in growing the business.

At what point did you feel that your business was established? After a tough third year when the recession really took hold we knew it was the time to change. In year four, the vision became clear of exactly what we needed to do to make this work. When we started we had 20 years' experience in the heating, plumbing and electrical industries and when Amelia joined us she brought her experience of 15 years in quality management, so we knew we had the wider skills to create the kind of business that would make a real difference to the lives of our customers. It's very scary to have such an ambitious vision but that's when you know that you've got something worth making that extra effort for.

We had always worked hard in the business but it wasn't until we started to see it in a different way that we knew we had the chance to build something bigger than the three of us, and something that could offer employment and training and really make an impact on other people's lives. That initial belief that we could do things better than other companies was the driver that influenced everything we did and we knew that we never wanted to compromise on that so we had to take some bold steps.

What were the major challenges affecting the growth of the business? Like so many businesses we were in a catch 22 situation for a long time. We were so busy with our existing clients that we never had a chance to really sit back and understand how to grow our business.

Then we decided that the answer was to do some marketing and we had a very simple, one-page website built and we produced a marketing strategy and started doing some networking and social media activity, but in some ways that just added to the frustration because we were getting enquiries and we still didn't have systems and processes in place to cope with them. We know we lost a lot of potential business because we were just too slow to react to enquiries. It was a big lesson for us. The three of us would have ad hoc discussions, usually when something went wrong and of course that meant that things got missed and it became more a case of 'working on the job' rather than managing and growing the company.

We knew we needed to collect and collate the correct information that would trigger more focused communications and discussion of the areas we needed to be improving in, but by not having management and financial tools in place we struggled to know exactly what we should be doing to improve things. When things get busy and tasks and deadlines build up, it's very easy to feel like you have lost control. Successful time management is key to making sure you can keep 'juggling those balls' and not let things slip.

How did you cope with having to manage the business instead of working in it? Letting go of working in the business is hard. It is like starting a new job all over again except the stakes are much higher. Working too much in the business greatly reduced office time causing late invoicing and delays in sending estimates. This was a major issue causing a yoyo effect in our monthly figures. However, the transition to employing other people and having the directors managing instead of directly producing revenue can cause a short-term drop in cash flow so the whole process has to be planned and managed really well.

Trying to find the right people to join the team as well as being able to afford it in a recession has been really tough. Do we employ unqualified people and invest in their training or employ qualified people and pay more salary? Do we outsource or subcontract and if we do, how do we ensure our high-quality standards are being met? This is an ongoing problem but we're getting there.

Our investor has been a great help in growing our management skills and we were recently lucky enough to join the government Growth Accelerator Service. Our expert coach has been (and still is) a great help, and we've finally got a three-year growth plan in place with monthly targets for the coming 12 months where we can measure our actual performance against our projections. We took the advice that this should be a living, breathing document that helps to inform all our decisions and we use it every day. It also forms the basis of our action plans and we now schedule meetings every week to discuss what worked and what didn't and to agree our action plans and targets for the coming week. Once a month we have a more formal directors' meeting and look at our progress and decide what needs to happen to keep us on track.

It's easy to beat yourself up when things go wrong (we never beat each other up!) but creating new habits takes time and when the pressure is on, you sometimes slip back to the old way of doing things just because it seems quicker and easier. When that happens, having the big picture and the plan to get there is invaluable and you just have to dust yourself off and get back to doing what is going to create the future you really want. Unfortunately, there is no quick fix to running a successful business. You need to experience failure to recognise the right paths to success.

What is your vision for the business? In terms of our service to customers, to be one of the few, or maybe the only company, that offers a full, comprehensive, one-stop shop for heating products, from a standard gas boiler to bespoke renewable heating solutions and, no matter how big we get, to work to the very highest standards with complete transparency so that we build on our reputation for always offering the very best long-term benefit to our customers. In terms of our personal philosophy and beliefs, we want to build the business to provide a great place to work and to develop people to their full potential. We haven't got a specific exit plan in mind but we do understand that a business that can run without its owners being involved on a day-to-day basis is more valuable than one that needs us to make all the decisions so we're definitely working towards that.

What is the most useful piece of advice you had when you started? Know your numbers! One of the things our coach mentioned when she first started working with us was that this is quite unusual and the fact that we know our margins and can accurately predict profits based on the number of jobs and the number of employees is the thing that is most likely to help us to reach our goal.

What tip would you offer someone who is making the transition from starting out to growing their business? You need to have a complete change in the way you think – from being self-employed and creating a job for yourself to creating and managing a business that can run without you. As mentioned above, it's vital to know your numbers, really control your cash flow, get your systems and processes in place and make yourself accountable to someone to do the things you say you'll do – and ask for help because you can't be an expert in everything. When you're always busy doing the urgent things that you're comfortable with you can use that as an excuse to never get around to doing the important ones that are unfamiliar and sometimes scary, but they're the ones that will make the difference between staying where you are and making real progress.

6

Managing marketing

Marketing, along with technology, is one of the areas of business that is changing more rapidly than any other. In this chapter you'll learn:

► what to do before you start marketing

► about marketing myths

► how to work out a marketing budget

► how to create a marketing strategy

► marketing tactics

► how to create a marketing plan

► the future of marketing.

What to do before you start marketing

Most people look to marketing as a solution when they want to grow their business, but before diving in, and especially before spending a lot of time and money, do check out other solutions first. Adjusting pricing, taking care of cash flow and improving customer service and sales techniques are all things that significantly contribute to business growth. Learning how to sell is particularly important as, without that, all the marketing in the world will make very little difference. Learning to sell and, particularly, how to negotiate, could save you a lot of time and money.

Write down six things you can do to increase revenue before you start marketing.

1................................ 4................................

2................................ 5................................

3................................ 6................................

Marketing myths

We are surrounded by marketing messages. We see and hear hundreds every day and probably don't notice half of them. Of those we do notice, it may be because they're funny, unusual, annoying or are endorsed by a celebrity that we admire or detest.

All of this means that even if we notice a marketing message, it doesn't mean we'll buy the product or service it is promoting. Big brands spend millions of pounds with agencies that compete with each other to produce the most noticed campaigns. Creative campaigns win awards for the agencies but that doesn't mean they win sales for the client. This is one of the biggest myths of marketing. A good example is the campaign for the 2015 IKEA catalogue. It is a short film that mimics the way the Apple Corporation promotes its new products. It is very clever, very funny and millions of people have watched it ('It's not an e-book or an i-book, it's a book-book'). Does this mean more people will order the IKEA catalogue? Maybe. IKEA could measure the number of catalogues ordered in 2015 compared to previous years and attribute it to this campaign. Does this mean more people will buy from IKEA in 2015? Who knows? And if they do, how do you measure the effect of this one campaign?

The messages that make us buy are linked with our desires or interests. We stop and look, watch or listen and we remember the message so that we choose that particular product or service over all others. We skim to see what speaks to or connects with our core wants, desires and values. That's why engagement is such a hot topic in marketing today but even engagement isn't enough by itself. Many 'viral' campaigns are heavily engineered and seeded with strategies that help them to spread. Viral should mean something that spreads quickly and uncontrollably but what usually happens is that an agency will pay for PR and placement on strategic websites or with 'influencers' to get it noticed. Engagement is high but that doesn't mean that sales will follow.

Marketing gets consumers stimulated to buy or investigate your product.

Marketing that really helps your business, rather than the business of the marketing agency, doesn't just offer the right product to the right consumer. It gets them emotionally stimulated to buy or at least investigate your product or service.

How to work out a marketing budget

This all comes down to knowing the value of a sale and the lifetime value of a customer.

If you make a gross profit of £80 on a sale, you may think that spending £100 to acquire one new customer is not worth it. However, if a customer is likely to bring you £80 profit every few months and, typically, stays with you for several years, then spending £100 to get one new customer is definitely worth it.

The following are some of the things to take into account when measuring the cost effectiveness of marketing:

Lead generation	Getting prospects into the start of the sales process. How much does it cost per lead?
Conversion rate	The percentage of people that are converted from leads to paying customers. (If this is low it means your lead generation process needs to be more closely targeted.)
Customer acquisition cost	How much money it takes to get a new customer from lead generation to order.
Lifetime value of a customer	The average amount of time a customer stays with you multiplied by the average spend per customer.
Monthly/annual recurring revenue	The average amount of money your customers are billed on a monthly or annual basis.

Some established businesses typically spend 5–7 per cent of their overall sales on marketing. New businesses often spend 20–30 per cent in the first two years and then scale back to an average of 7–10 per cent annually.

The budget is typically split between:

1   brand development costs (which includes all the channels you use to promote your brand such as your website, blogs, printed collateral, etc.)

2   the costs of promoting your business (campaigns, advertising, events, etc.).

Measure and adjust

There are no guarantees that any particular type of marketing will work as there are so many variables to consider, some of which will be out of your control, e.g. world events, economic situations, the weather, what your competitors are doing, etc. Most marketing is about trying something and measuring the result. The ultimate goal should be to increase your marketing return on investment by reducing the cost of customer acquisition. Stay focused on increasing the number and quality of leads.

Before reading any further, decide on the way you will set your marketing budget, based on what you can really afford and not on vague promises of return on investment. It is easier to ramp up a strategy that is working than to recover money that has been wasted.

> How will you set your marketing budget for the next 12 months?

How to create a marketing strategy

Your marketing strategy is an explanation of the goals you need to achieve with your marketing efforts (the WHAT). It is shaped by your business goals. It's not uncommon for people to confuse a marketing strategy with a marketing plan. This could include:

▶ more customers

▶ more sales

▶ more sales per customer

▶ more profit per customer

▶ reduce the cost of acquiring new customers

▶ extend the lifetime value of customers

▶ launch a new product

▶ increase market share

▶ break into a new market.

The marketing plan is HOW you are going to achieve those marketing goals. It's the application of the strategy – a roadmap that will guide you from one point to another.

When it comes to marketing, it's vital to identify the WHAT before deciding on the HOW. Strategy is about the thinking and planning is about the doing.

The following questions will help you to define your strategy. They are fundamental to your business planning and you may have already answered them elsewhere. If not, now is a good time to do it!

Strategy is about the thinking and planning is about the doing.

Business

▶ What business are you in?

▶ What compelled you to start this business?

▶ What is the market size (by geography, by industry etc.)?

▶ Are there any key industry trends that affect your success?

Service/product

▶ Does your product/service satisfy a need or a want?

▶ What features/benefits are associated with your product/service?

▶ Of those features/benefits which, if any, make you different from your competitors?

▶ What improvements can you make to better meet your customer needs?

▶ How important is price in the decision to buy?

▶ What is the current process for selling (promoting) your product/ service?

▶ Is the decision to buy impulse or planned?

Customers (current, prospect, target)

▶ What market segments are you targeting?

▶ Do your customers have any issues or concerns when buying a service/ product like yours?

▶ Can you understand more about your customers? Who are they and where are they?

▶ What does your identified target audience know and believe about you today?

▶ What is the single most important message you must communicate to them?

Competitors

▶ What categories of competition threaten your success (direct and indirect)?

▶ Who are the competitors in those categories (by service/product)?

▶ Which competitors have the biggest market share and greatest brand awareness with your target audience(s) – are they the same?

Use the answers to these questions to come up with a very clear strategy, i.e what you want to achieve from your marketing. This should be reviewed regularly along with your business objectives.

Marketing tactics

Some of the tactics you can choose from include:

▶ advertising

▶ pay per click

▶ Google ad words

▶ email newsletters

▶ direct mail

▶ text (SMS) messages

▶ mobile apps and footfall check-ins

▶ referrals

▶ word of mouth

▶ social media

▶ website traffic

▶ search engine optimisation (SEO)

▶ business networking

▶ cold calling

▶ trade associations

▶ seminars

▶ promotional events

▶ sponsoring (events, charities)

▶ presentations

▶ talks and demos

▶ trade shows

▶ exhibitions.

Marketing collateral is the term used to describe printed material that helps to re-enforce branding. Brochures, compliment slips, business cards, letterheads and sometimes giveaways such as branded pens, mugs, key fobs and mouse mats are part of this.

There's such a wide variety of tactics on offer, it can be tempting to just dive in and pick whatever you like the sound of or have been exposed to previously. Don't be misled by 'free' options like social media. They are time consuming and need to be treated in a very different way to other 'traditional' marketing tactics.

Before deciding on tactics, ask yourself the following:

▶ Does it fit with your marketing strategy?

▶ Will it achieve your marketing goals?

▶ Does it appeal to the audience you are targeting?

▶ Does it fit with your brand image?

▶ Can you afford to do it regularly and consistently?

▶ Do you have the time and resources to do it?

▶ Can you do it within your marketing budget?

▶ Do you have the skill set to do what's needed?

Typical marketing mix: inbound vs outbound

A typical marketing mix for a small business consists of a few main elements that fall in either inbound or outbound marketing categories.

Inbound	Outbound
Website	Advertising online
Email campaigns*	Billboards, TV, radio
Social media	Print
Blog	Direct mail
Forums	Collateral (brochures, leaflets, etc.)
Pay per click	Trade shows
Search engine optimisation	Conferences
Videos	Seminars
Demos	Cold calling/telemarketing
Webinars	Public relations

* Email marketing can be both inbound and outbound. Email is inbound when it is used to attract highly qualified leads organically, and outbound when used to reach out to targeted prospects.

Both inbound and outbound marketing methods have their advantages and disadvantages, so it's a good idea to blend both into your marketing strategy.

Content marketing

Content marketing is about recognising that consumers regularly avoid advertising and 'interruption' marketing techniques and instead prefer to 'discover' information about products and services that they are thinking of buying.

By creating and distributing valuable, relevant and consistent content it is possible to attract and acquire a clearly defined audience and then convert them into profitable customers.

Basically, content marketing is the art of communicating with your customers and prospects without selling. Instead of pitching your products or services, you are delivering information that makes your buyer better informed.

Content marketing is being used by some of the greatest marketing organisations in the world, including P&G, Microsoft, Cisco Systems and John Deere. It's also developed and executed by small businesses and one-person shops around the globe.

When you produce content you will naturally post it on your website, blog, Google Plus page, YouTube channel etc. However, it is important to place content in places where your customers are most likely to see it and by observing where the key influencers place their content you could get valuable clues about where to post yours.

It is also important to have mechanisms to collect information on the people who like your content. Facebook 'likes' are useless but a mailing list of people who have signed up to get regular blog posts, download some information or get free tips is hugely valuable and gives you the opportunity to market to those people on a regular basis as they have given you permission to do so.

Social media marketing

In Chapter Four – Managing social media, we looked at how to manage social media generally, but social media marketing is a topic that threatens to eclipse all other social media activities, despite being the one that is least likely to yield results. (E-mail marketing produces seven times more results than social media marketing.)

As soon as large numbers of people started turning up on social networks like Twitter and Facebook, marketers saw it as an opportunity to reach ever bigger markets and social media marketing was born. Most people in the social media world have been practising for less than two years and many have little experience of marketing or business generally. It is an area where the uninitiated can be taken advantage of very easily. Measuring the return on investment on social media marketing is a hot topic. Reports show that over 60 per cent of small businesses get zero results from social media marketing and that 95 per cent of big brands (spending millions) are unhappy with their results.

The next big change in this area is that businesses are moving from trying to be engaging and social with their customers (marketing by stealth) and using more authentic ways to add real value to their transactions. The user experience will be the most important thing to be taken into account in this new wave of marketing via social networks. What is clear is that users are so adept at ignoring interruptions to their social networking that traditional marketing doesn't work in this medium and claims need to be treated with a great deal of caution.

Influencer marketing

There are several social media tools that claim to identify influencers but most are limited and some are deeply flawed. Klout, Kred and PeerIndex are the most well-known and are used by some large B2C brands like airlines and hotel chains resulting in upgrades for those seen as influencers in these markets. There are many other tools, but the advantage that small businesses have is that they can usually identify these influencers from their own knowledge.

Trying to reach everyone in your target market and hoping to hit some of them is a time-consuming, money-eating, ineffective way of doing things. The alternative is to identify and follow the influencers within your market place and to get their attention in the hope that they will become your advocates.

According to Keller and Berry in their book *The Influentials*, influencers fall into five loose categories:

1   **Activists**: get involved with their communities, political movements, charities etc.

2   **Connected**: have large social networks.

3   **Impact**: are looked up to and are trusted by others.

4   **Active minds**: have multiple and diverse interests.

5   **Trendsetters**: tend to be early adopters (or leavers) in markets.

A model for identifying influencers has been developed by Influencer50:

▶   **Market reach.** The number of people an individual has the ability to connect with. This is not just about their online influence but about their influence in the world, for example, people with a high personal profile (celebrities, film stars, sporting heroes, politicians etc.) In the online world, this could include high-profile bloggers and journalists with large followings.

▶   **Independence**. Whether an influencer has a vested interest in pro-moting a particular point of view.

▶ **Frequency of impact**. The number of opportunities an individual has to influence buying decisions. People who are always in the public eye, for the right reasons, score most highly. For example, a celebrity footballer is in the news almost every week but a James Bond star usually has influence for a short time when a new film is released. Online, you need people who are frequent, consistent users of social media and whose content is widely shared.

▶ **Expertise**. How much of an expert is the influencer.

▶ **Persuasiveness**. The consequences of ignoring an influencer's advice.

▶ **Thoroughness of role**. The extent to which influence is exerted across the decision lifecycle. If your product or service is seasonal it has a short buying decision lifecycle. If a customer buys from you every week or only once in three years, the people who can influence those buying decisions will be very different.

'Social influence' gets a lot of attention in the social media world and Google is giving more weight to 'social liking' of web pages, blog posts and social networking posts, especially those that have a Google +1 tag. However, the huge majority of people influence each other face to face rather than through online channels like blogs and social networks. People trust face-to-face friends most, with a recent survey showing 73 per cent have near or complete trust in people they regularly meet versus just 33 per cent in online friends. They may communicate with these friends online but they are trusted more because they are friends in real life.

> **The huge majority of people influence each other face to face rather than through online channels.**

If you choose to engage with an influencer directly, you need to understand what they are currently writing and talking about, what their interests are and, over time, build a relationship such that the influencer may choose to review your product or service which could lead to some excellent publicity and exposure.

Using this information, start to think of the influencers in your market and the routes you can use to reach them. This could include both online and offline activity, from traditional press releases, events with VIP guests, samples of products to review, interviews and seeking their opinion to reading and commenting on their blog, engaging them in conversation on Twitter, liking and sharing their Facebook or Google Plus posts and engaging in discussions with them on LinkedIn.

Marketing automation

Marketing automation is software that works in conjunction with web-based services to execute, manage and automate marketing tasks and processes. It replaces manual and repetitive marketing processes with purpose-built software geared to performance.

Because it works, marketing automation software (MA) is now being increasingly used to track and manage these complex customer behavioural processes, wherever and whenever a contact occurs.

Marketing automation is ideal for delivering the right content at the 'moments of truth' in a buyer's journey whether it is an email, download or webinar. And when MA is integrated with existing CRM systems, the combination provides a joined-up, end-to-end process capable of delivering streams of good quality leads to the sales department.

Below are some good questions to ask yourself when deciding if marketing automation is the right move for your business.

- ▶ Are you generating a steady flow of new and qualified leads?
- ▶ Are you overwhelmed with the number of quality leads you need to follow up?
- ▶ Do you have an efficient content strategy mapped to your buyer's journey?
- ▶ Are you tracking your leads' digital journey across every touch point and marketing channel (not just email)?
- ▶ Do you have a proven lead nurturing strategy that you want to scale?

These are all good signs that marketing automation (when done right) could work for your business.

There are two key principles to keep in mind when developing a strategy that scales and evolves with your customers:

1   Marketing automation does not do marketing and lead generation for you, but can help scale your successful efforts.

2   Marketing messages should be centred on the real, live person at the receiving end of your campaigns.

This means you should treat them like a real whole person with information gathered from different tools like email, social media, etc. If we can leverage all the marketing tools, channels and behavioural data possible to paint a complete picture of a person, we can nurture them based on their unique challenges and interests, not based solely on the emails they open or click through.

Mobile marketing

Much of the marketing we've talked about revolves around your website. Most printed material will have a web address included and social media links will drive people back to your website. Even if you have a physical venue, shop or outlet, people are more likely to look up your website before they come visiting.

> **Even if you have a physical shop, people are more likely to look up your website before visiting.**

They are also more likely to do this on a smartphone or tablet than any other way so you must be sure that your website is not only appealing, has some strong calls to action and tells a great story but that it does it all for people on the move and displays your information in a way that responds to different sizes of screen (responsive websites).

More and more businesses are recognising that they also need a mobile app (application software) to encourage more research or online buying. More mobile subscribers use apps than browse the web on their devices. This trend is predicted to increase over the next few years.

Marketing by SMS (Short Message Service) or text is also on the increase and means that mobile phone numbers are rapidly replacing email addresses as the most valuable marketing information – which is why Facebook bought SMS service WhatsApp for $19 billion!

How to create a marketing plan

There are many sample marketing plans available, but this is one of the best we've come across, kindly supplied by Jon Buscall of Jontus Media. For your business, take the same headings and use these examples to complete your own Marketing Plan.

Note from Jon: *'This marketing plan is yours to adapt and tweak as necessary. Where possible I've included examples based on a fictional dog trainer.'* (Jon is a devoted basset hound fan!)

Your model marketing plan

Author:

Date prepared:

Marketing plan summary

Summarise the contents of your plan in one or two paragraphs so any reader of your plan can get the gist of the document. Note: Do this AFTER you've written the rest of the document!

Company overview

Start by providing a brief company overview. For example:

▶ dog-training business

▶ based in Brighton

▶ established 2011

▶ key service offers:

    ▶ individual training

    ▶ bad behaviour consultations

    ▶ puppy classes

    ▶ ring training.

Unique selling proposition

What makes you stand out from your competition? For example:

▶ Accredited canine behaviourist Anna Graham provides one-to-one consultations for dog owners in Brighton.

Value to the customer

Think through the things you want the customer to value about your products, services, what you offer or do, etc. For example:

- ▶ highly qualified trainer
- ▶ provides follow-up Skype consultations where necessary
- ▶ trust: ten years' experience working with the local animal hospital.

Summary of goals and objectives

Where does the business need to go, helped by this marketing plan?
For example:

- ▶ Anna seeks to increase her client base to enable the hiring of a junior consultant
- ▶ gain media exposure
- ▶ sign a book deal
- ▶ specialise more on problem behaviour consultations.

The market

Take time to do market research into any new innovations in the market, customer trends, new actors entering the market, etc. Perform a SWOT (Strengths, Weaknesses, Opportunities, Threats) analysis of your business. This section takes time!

For example, this is how Anna Graham, our dog trainer, may complete her own SWOT Analysis:

Strengths

- ▶ highly qualified
- ▶ recommended by vets
- ▶ up-to-date on new developments in positive training.

Weaknesses

- ▶ no marketing experience

▶

- ▶ no website
- ▶ no car on Fridays.

Opportunities

- ▶ first dog trainer to offer Skype consultations in the area
- ▶ a new animal hospital opening in the region
- ▶ upswing in families in the region with pet dogs
- ▶ approaching the summer when families want new pets.

Threats

- ▶ five established behaviourists already working in the area
- ▶ puppy classes increasingly offered by dog day-care centres.

Competitor overview

Competitors

- ▶ Specify the top five to ten.
- ▶ Take time to research three key aspects of the business.

Competitor	Value proposition	Strengths	Weaknesses
Jo Whittaker	Behaviour consultations for large-breed dogs.	Well known as featured in the media. Highly skilled.	Poor website. Overly focused on social media.

Marketing overview up to present

Specify the staff currently working on marketing and sales or those you intend to use if this is your first plan. For example:

Current sales and marketing personnel

- ▶ Diane Barnard – webmaster

▶ Peter Madsen – print/web design

▶ Anna Graham (business owner) – content creation

Target audience: brand archetypes/brand personas

Really try and understand the kind of person you are targeting. The more you know about them, the more you can target content to them and put it in the places that they'll find it. For example, dog trainer, Anna Graham's target audience may be:

1 Busy mother

▶ 30–45

▶ loves dogs

▶ well-educated

▶ focuses on running a busy household and a career

▶ wants perfection

▶ spends a lot of money on household furnishings

▶ drives a nice car

▶ lives between Brighton and Lewes

▶ checks Facebook regularly

▶ on Instagram.

Marketing channels

Decide whether these are existing or planned for the future. For example:

▶ website

▶ Facebook

▶ Twitter

▶ etc.

Website

If you have an existing website, provide an overview of how it is performing. For example:

▶

▶ Website.com is the hub of Anna's content marketing campaign. The site informs ... New leads are brought into the site via Google Search (SEO), paid advertising (both digital and traditional) and social media referral.

▶ Website.com gets on average 25,000 visitors per month, with 10,000 visits come from search traffic.

▶ The site has a 0.5% bounce rate (i.e. visitors who leave the site in under one second), which is extremely good. Typically, sites have a bounce rate of over 50%+

▶ Social media (Facebook, Twitter, LinkedIn) generates approximately 25% of all traffic to the website.

▶ A further 23% is direct traffic: i.e. those who know the URL or have it bookmarked.

▶ 2% of traffic comes from paid advertising.

▶ A content marketing strategy, implemented since April 2013, involves regularly publishing and updating the site with news, pictures, audio and video which not only enables Anna to get her key messages out to the community but also provides a snapshot of life as a trainer as she is hoping to recruit a junior partner.

▶ The content that is published aims to ... etc.

▶ Content is created and published across Anna's marketing channels and is geared towards each segment of the target audience. The site includes a variety of text, audio and video content, designed to appeal to different users who prefer to consume different types of content.

▶ Regular updates and ongoing search engine optimisation are essential to appear at the top of Google search results: e.g. ...

Social media

Decide how social media will work for you. For example, Anna will use social media to:

▶ drive traffic to the website.com (currently 25% of all monthly traffic to the main site comes from social media)

▶ engage with the local community

▶ build new relationships with the different segments of target audience

▶ increase brand recognition.

Typically, mothers follow or engage with Anna on the largest social media channels. Facebook and Pinterest are particularly useful for reaching mothers between ages 35–55.

Traffic to Anna's Facebook page remains fairly constant although changes to the Facebook algorithm has made it harder to reach our audience without investing in so-called 'boosted' (i.e. paid promotional) posts.

Facebook adverts enable Anna to target niche markets: i.e. geographic regions, different age groups, etc.

Monitoring and measurement activities

Specify when and how you plan/or currently measure your marketing metrics. For example:

Channel	Date of review	Method of measurement	Outcomes	Ongoing goals
Website (inc. blog)	Weekly	Google analytics	Increased site traffic during course of year.	To improve sales funnel; build community.
Podcast	Monthly	Download stats	Increased traffic, growth. Downloads.	To increase growth; increase shares on social media.
Facebook	Weekly	FB Metrics; Raven Tools analysis	Increased growth in Likes increasing, but diminished reach (approx 25%) since Facebook changed its algorithm.	To increase Likes; to increase traffic to site and elicit bookings.
Twitter	Weekly	Hootsuite analytics	Increased growth, reach, tweets. Increased number of click-throughs to business website.	To increase followers; increase traffic to website and connect with local dog owners.

▶

Current key performance indicators

Specify some key indicators that you have noted for the period you are measuring. For example:

▶ Based on a comparison of months in two successive years, traffic to website.com is relatively stable with approximately 850 visitors to the site each day.

▶ Approximately one in three visitors to website.com are new visitors.

▶ Visitors to website.com in comparison period 1 on average clicked through 1.73 pages compared to 4.15 in comparison period 2.

▶ The previous website had a bounce rate (i.e. the percentage of visitors who left within under a second) of 68.03%; the current website's bounce rate is 0.24%.

Goals for next measurement period

Decide what your goals are for the next measurement period. For example:

▶ Increase weekly podcast downloads 15%.

▶ Increase site traffic by 15%.

Goals for following measurement period

For example:

▶ Have 100 subscribers to an email list.

▶ Increase weekly podcast downloads by 15%.

▶ Increase site traffic by 15%.

Planned marketing activities

Think about what marketing activities you will undertake in the future. For example:

▶ Continue digital content marketing strategies alongside paid print media advertising.

▶ Increase paid digital marketing on channels like Facebook, local pet store websites given the demonstrable success hitherto.

> ▶ Develop more quality content marketing materials: (e.g. videos, ebooks, learning materials, infographics) to stand out from the competition and connect in new, deeper ways with each segment of the target audience.
>
> *Source:* Jon Buscall, Jontus Media, **www.jontusmedia.com**

The future of marketing

Trust is the biggest factor in any transaction. If your marketing is utterly transparent and authentic this will not be a problem. Trying to hide anything in these days of internet searches and social media is a recipe for disaster.

People want to be noticed and to feel that any marketing message is directed specifically at them personally, that you truly understand their problems and needs and can make their life better:

Trust is the biggest factor in any transaction.

▶ Personalised emails (addressing people by name), improve click-through rates by 14 per cent, and conversion rates by 10 per cent. Personalised content (addressing issues specific to that reader) get even better results.

▶ In a study of 650 multi-channel marketing campaigns, personalised campaigns consistently and overwhelmingly beat static campaigns in generating a high response rate from recipients.

▶ A recommendation from a trusted friend conveying a relevant message is up to 50 times more likely to trigger a purchase than any other recommendation.

▶ 75 per cent of people prefer to receive offers over any other form of call-to-action.

▶ 59 per cent of B2B marketers say email is the most effective channel for generating revenue and 49 per cent of B2B marketers spend more time and resources on email than on other channels.

In short, it's not about blasting out messages. What it is about is finding a way to improve the targeting of your messages to improve the user experience while benefiting your business.

Fashion chain Tokyo Girls collects so much information on its fans that it can send targeted text messages that are so highly personalised that they get a 46 per cent conversion to sales – a previously unheard of conversion rate. The text message will be something like, 'Hi Jane, we know how much you like Rhianna and the dress she wore to the MOBO awards. We have it in your size and you can get it at 20% discount if you order by midnight tonight!'

Next steps

▶ Define a specific marketing strategy.

▶ Come up with ideas to personalise your offering.

▶ Work out your marketing budget.

▶ Complete your model marketing plan.

▶ Create a simple marketing routine that addresses the kinds of marketing activities that can be done on a daily, weekly, monthly and quarterly basis. Pick and choose ideas from the following suggestions.

Daily

Select the social media channels that you know your customers use. Deliver content that you know your target market will engage with and that will draw them to your website. Engage directly (i.e. have a conversation) with customers, prospects or influencers.

Weekly

If you have a blog, weekly updates are the most preferred option for most subscribers. Short and sharp is better than long and rambling. Blog posts based on the questions your clients or prospects ask are great for attracting readers and also good for SEO.

Send a handwritten note card to a couple of clients or prospects every week. In these digital days a handwritten note really stands out.

Update content on your website, particularly anything with dates. Google will like this a lot, as will your customers.

Monthly

Sending out an email newsletter once a month gives you an opportunity to touch your clients and prospects and keep your name at the top of their minds. Select a target date like the 15th of each month to manage expectation. There are lots of great free tools for designing and scheduling newsletters.

Run a monthly campaign where you focus on a certain product or service, or a certain target market.

Run a competition on your website or blog.

Start a weekly or monthly chat on Twitter or Facebook or a Google Plus Hangout all with the aim of showcasing your expertise and generating leads.

Quarterly

If you are a good public speaker seek out opportunities at networking events, exhibitions or trade shows.

Send out a press release and seek out PR opportunities on radio, TV, podcasts or interviews in appropriate magazines.

Pitch an article concept to appropriate outlets.

Annually

Organise a client appreciation event. Work with a few strategic partners. The idea here is for each of you to invite some of your best clients as well as a few prospects and you can use this event to highlight those clients who've had exceptional results to entice others to want to work with you and your partners as well.

Marketing is really about developing the 'know, like, and trust factor' and that doesn't happen overnight. Marketing has to take place on a routine and regular basis for it to be successful because it takes time and multiple touches.

CASE STUDY
SnoozeShade

Cara Sayer is the Founder and MD of SnoozeShade a company that provides practical and useful products that make life with a baby easier. She describes herself as Chief Sleep Officer after her first product was inspired by inventing a shade for her daughter's buggy to make it easier for her to sleep while out and about. Cara wanted an easy-to-use, lightweight and safe equivalent to a blackout blind for the pushchair and when she complained about not being able to find any, her friends suggested she should make one. The rest, as they say, is history.

The business was started in 2004 and it took about 18 months before the first product was manufactured and ready for delivery. Cara used her own savings to start the business and now turns over £250,000. The business doesn't employ anyone but uses a team of freelancers in various parts of the business.

We caught up with Cara at the end of a trip to a trade fair in Australia.

How did you go about starting production? I approached a company that I knew were used to making baby-safe products as they supplied cover-mounted products on the front of baby magazines.

What experience did you bring to the business? I had never been in retail, manufacture or run my own business – so to be honest it was all a huge learning curve (and still is).

At what point did you feel that your business was established? When we started delivering to major retailers such as John Lewis, Mothercare and JoJoMamanBebe. Sometimes I still have to pinch myself.

What have been your most successful marketing tactics? I have always invested a lot of time into social media – Facebook and Twitter especially – and we have very active communities and followings.

What has been your biggest challenges? To control fast growth and keep on top of the business. Cash flow is always a challenge when you have to place high-value orders for product – and forecasting is always a finger in the air effort as there is no magic formula (sadly). It relies on experience and being prepared to take educated risks. Being the mother to a small child had its own unique challenges as I was the primary caregiver and my husband was also working full-time and couldn't help and we didn't have the money (or inclination) for a nanny. This meant lots of working through the night and reliance on my mother to help me with my daughter while I worked. Without my mother's support I wouldn't be here today in a professional (or personal) capacity.

How did you cope with having to manage the business instead of working in it? I didn't – I work in it and I run it.

What is your vision for the business? I'd like to build SnoozeShade until it's a really well recognised brand (we're getting there already) and then look for a larger business that can take it over and grow it further than I can.

What is the most useful piece of advice you had when you started? Get your pricing and margins right from the start. It can be hard to put right if you've not worked out your sums.

What tip would you offer someone who is making the transition from starting out to growing their business? Don't over order stock in the early days – better to pay more and buy less and sell what you have first. Don't be scared of taking risks but make sure you have money to invest that you can afford to lose. It costs money to grow a business and be prepared to work harder and longer than you ever have before in your life.

7

Managing sales

Managing sales is an ongoing, continuous process. If it gets to the point where you urgently need to create more sales, it's probably already too late.

In this chapter we'll look at:

▶ CRM systems

▶ the sales funnel

▶ what you are really selling

▶ the emotion of buying

▶ sales conversations

▶ getting more sales per customer

▶ your pricing strategy

▶ how listening is an essential sales skill

▶ how to define your sales proposition

▶ social selling

▶ hiring sales people

▶ the fear of turning down a sale.

Small businesses often shy away from selling through fear of seeming pushy. Instead, they spend disproportionate amounts of time and money on marketing without following up on opportunities. The thing that makes a BIG difference to your bottom line is learning how to sell. With social selling the pushy pitch is redundant because the conversation is all about the prospect.

> **Learning how to sell will make a big difference to your bottom line.**

The tools that have been developed to help businesses take advantage of the phenomena of social networking are a salesperson's best friend and many of them are free and easy to use – certainly easier and more effective than cold calling!

CRM systems

One of the most important tools in the sales process is a Contact Relationship Management system (CRM), from which there are many to choose. There are some very simple free ones, and some are very expensive and very sophisticated, but any CRM is better than none. That's worth saying again:

Any **CRM is better than none.**

Find a simple one that suits you and put it to work. You can always upgrade as your business grows and you think about linking the CRM to other systems.

In its simplest form a CRM system is software that helps to organise the sales leads that are produced by marketing activity. The business cards you collect at an exhibition or people you connect with on social networks, responses to offers, details of people who visit your website or sign up to your newsletter are all entered on the system with all of their contact details. The more sophisticated systems will fill in things like LinkedIn and Twitter accounts, enabling social networking contact as well as the more usual phone calls or email follow-ups.

When contact is made with a prospect, dates and details are entered with calendar notes for future follow-ups, notes about specific areas of interest in products or services, anniversary dates and anything else that makes it easy to connect and build a relationship. Of course, when a prospect becomes a customer, this information is used to manage the customer relationship and make sure that they stay with you as a happy and satisfied client who feels valued.

The sales funnel

The traditional sales funnel is a systematic process where you progressively filter your prospects into customers and further refine them into repeat or high-value customers. With the advent of sophisticated searches and social networks, there is some debate about whether this is still relevant.

It is quite likely that your prospective customer finds *you* and has already researched what you have to offer before you make the first move. In other words, you become the prospective supplier and the customer is firmly in charge of knowing what they want and where they want to enter into the sales process.

However, this doesn't completely rule out the process of attracting and qualifying people who may have an inclination to purchase your products or services. In most cases the qualification occurs when a person *opts-in* to receive something from you. It's this opting-in step that builds prospects, since they have just taken an action that indicates they have at least some desire for what you offer.

Buying lists is rarely successful. Unless someone has actively given you permission to approach them they'll resend it and ask to be taken off the list.

Hot leads

Opportunities

Proposals/quotes

New customers

The sales funnel

Here are some examples of how to attract people into a sales funnel:

▶ Offer free information (e.g., blog posts, white papers, ebooks, newsletters, webinars) in return for contact details.

▶ Organise free networking events or seminars.

▶ Offer free trials of goods or services (take the puppy home and if, after 30 days you don't like it, you can bring it back).

▶ Organise competitions but only if the prize is directly related to your product or service.

So long as the content you provide is good and does what you promise, this will help to convince your prospect that your business is worth forming a relationship with. That relationship becomes stronger as customers accept more free offerings, and then start to purchase and learn to trust and appreciate what you do.

What strategy will you adopt to attract people into your sales funnel?

What are the stages you will lead them through to buy your highest priced goods or services?

Managing qualified but not-ready-to-buy leads in advance of an active sales process is an important activity. The justification is clear – the more actively you can nurture leads and build long-term relationships based on trust and credibility, well before the prospect is ready to buy, the more likely you are to win the business and increase your conversion rates over time.

The more actively you can nurture leads and build long-term relationships, the more likely you are to win the business.

What's more, effectively nurturing leads can significantly decrease your marketing budget for new leads over time.

Selling is all about TRUST

The main trait of marketing and sales in the late twentieth century was aggressive promotion that took little heed of the real needs of the customers. Consumers were prey and sales people predators. It's no wonder that many people were uncomfortable with this approach and, as business owners, we have the opportunity to change all that.

More and more businesses, large and small, are embracing openness and transparency, treating clients, customers, suppliers, employees and all stakeholders with equal respect and creating businesses that people are proud to work for, proud to supply, proud to invest in and proud to buy from. You may be selling online or from a physical location, you may be selling through advertisements or pay-per-click, or you may have that rare ability to sit face to face with a prospect and negotiate a deal, but the basis of all of these activities is trust.

Sales professionals like to distinguish the difference between the transactional and consultative approach to selling. Essentially this is the difference between the customer choosing what they want and the salesperson taking the order and the deeper relationship building process that allows the salesperson to explore the real needs of the customer and help them to choose the best solution.

The one thing that all of these sales techniques have in common is that TRUST is a prerequisite to every transaction. The trust can be in a brand or a company, in a payment system or a returns policy, or in the person who is attempting to make the sale. Establishing trust is absolutely imperative.

In Chapter One – Managing the business, we asked you to define the purpose of your business and this is why ...

When you are sure of your purpose and values, your business becomes a vehicle, not only for you but for all the people that are involved in it.

When you represent the bigger picture, you're not asking for a sale, you're asking people to share the world you're creating and when they buy, they're buying so much more than a simple service or product. They're not comparing prices, they're comparing value. If someone wonders if or why they should do business with you they should be in no doubt about what they can expect from you and, just as importantly, what you will expect from them.

What you are aiming for is to find the people who believe what you believe and who want to do business with you. If they don't share your values, they won't buy and that's a good thing because if they did, they'd become the customer from hell.

What you're aiming for is to turn customers into partners. Businesses that live and breathe their purpose don't need to spend a lot of time and resources advertising it.

Whatever sales approach you adopt, make sure that you are reflecting the values of your business.

We all knew that John Lewis, Waitrose and Marks & Spencer would not be involved in the horsemeat scandals of 2013 or other exploitative behaviour. Customers can see it for themselves, not from what the business says but from what it does.

Whatever sales approach you adopt you need to be sure that you are reflecting the values of your business, and, for long-term success that you are selling with integrity.

Points for selling with integrity

Simplicity: It is important to offer clear, concise communication to help your customer make the right choices.

Transparency: Your customer must feel you have nothing to hide, no hidden extras or obscure contract policies. They need to be sure you are offering them what they need, not what is best for you.

Responsibility: Today's consumers are highly receptive to supporting businesses that help the greater good. It's not just about being different, but about making a difference.

Sustainability: In the wider sense this is the ability to meet the needs of today without compromising tomorrow. It is also about making sure your solution will be something that gives lasting value.

Affordability: While it is not your responsibility to second guess whether your client can afford your services or products it isn't a good idea to tie them in to a deal that will cause problems down the line.

What are you really selling?

The words we use to describe our business, whether written or verbal, are key to letting potential customers know what we do. However, choosing the right words is an art form in itself. Sigmund Freud proved this when he once described the loving art of kissing as 'a contact between the mucous membrane of the lips of the two people concerned'!

Too often we focus our company description by listing the products and services we provide, rather than the more effective angle of how we help our customers. Take these two examples:

1 John Lewis

As traditional as mince pies and jingle bells, each Christmas John Lewis launches a much-hyped advert, backed up by a soundtrack that is almost guaranteed to provide the artist with a number one single. But what is the message that they're portraying? Is it a list of their new ranges that are available? Is it the brands that they stock? No and no! In the words of Craig Inglis, its marketing director, its aim is to 'connect emotionally with our customers'.

2 Disneyland Paris

Every year we see a collection of multimedia adverts for Europe's largest theme park, but rarely an image of one of their rides. Are they not proud of the services they provide? Of course they are. However, by showing excited children and happy, smiling parents, they create the feeling that visiting Disney is a memorable experience for the entire family.

To relate this to our own businesses, we need to look more at how our products or services benefit our customers, rather than what the offering does.

The emotion of buying

All buying decisions are emotional so in order to be good at selling, you need to know exactly what emotion your customer is going to experience. Most businesses are started to solve a problem and a few create delight.

All buying decisions are emotional.

Do your customers have a pain they need your solution to alleviate or do they have an irrational passion for something that you can supply?

It's not always as obvious as it might seem. It all comes down to what you are really selling.

These three famous brands seem to have it nailed, but what do you think they're really selling?

Revlon sells ...

Harley Davidson sells ...

Nike sells ...

On the face of it Revlon could be seen to be solving the problem of imperfect skin or ageing. Harley Davidson might have started by solving a transport problem or a delight in speed or high quality machinery and Nike is solving the need that sports people have for high performance equipment and garments. However, according to their own PR, Revlon sells hope, Harley Davidson sells freedom and Nike sells winning.

What is the emotion that you are really selling?

Write down a list of words or phrases that describe the benefits of your products or services. You could even try answering this question from the perspective of the people that you're targeting: What's in it for me?

Use these words to create a sentence or two that you can then use to describe your business in networking events or on your website.

Expert opinion Richard Young, Managing Director of Pipeliner CRM

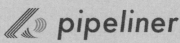

Getting into the sales conversation

People buy from people they know, like and trust.

This is a well-documented fact and means that one of your key objectives when meeting with prospects is to build rapport so you can earn the likability factor.

Make it all about them

It's human nature, but people like to talk about themselves! When you're interacting with a customer, use open-ended questions to encourage the customer to talk about themselves.

Small talk is a good place to start because it can help you find common ground and topics where you share a common interest (and people like people who are like themselves). As a result, common ground is great for building that initial rapport and establishing a foundation of trust.

It's about how you make them FEEL

Questions are really effective at creating an experience for your customer.

We've all been in conversations with people who drain our energy, don't make us feel good, and leave us willing the interaction to end – FAST! In comparison, we've also been around people who make us feel good, comfortable, and as a result we're happy to talk freely.

Anyone who is selling wants the latter. You want to make a prospect feel at ease so they are willing to share information with you. For sure you don't want a customer to feel manipulated, but if you can encourage them to volunteer the insights and information you need to progress with the sale, you're more likely to successfully nudge a customer along your pipeline.

Don't assume

Never hold back on asking a question because you think you know the answer, and don't be afraid of asking a question because you think it's silly.

Assumptions are dangerous things, especially if you end up basing your pitch and the rest of the conversation on something that you assume a customer is already familiar with.

You may be afraid of asking a question because you think it's silly or something you should already know. To overcome this, do your research first. It's always best to go into an interaction with a customer with a good understanding of the business – but feel free to check your understanding (whilst demonstrating you have done your homework).

▶

Focus on your customer's pains

Customers are NOT interested in the features of your product (even if you think they're really cool!). All they are interested in is how your product/service is going to make their life easier, by helping them overcome the challenges they face.

That's why you need to be really clear on what is causing your customer pain.

▶ What is playing on their mind and keeping them up at night?

▶ What one thing will transform their life if they can resolve it?

▶ What motivates them?

When you know your customer's pain, you can tailor your pitch to demonstrate how you can help them solve it. When you have the insight and information that enables you to do that, your relevancy soars. That's because no longer are you seen as an annoying salesperson. Instead, you are perceived as someone who can genuinely help and add value.

What are they looking for help with?

Once you know why your customer needs you, you can help.

In fact, helping is the quickest route to selling.

Resist the temptation to talk solely about how your product/service can assist. Instead, aim to help your prospect discover ways to overcome the issues they're facing. Obviously, this will require you to have a broader range of knowledge, BUT if you can do this, you'll reposition yourself. Instead of just being a salesperson, sharing these wider insights can help you be perceived as a trusted adviser.

Getting more sales per customer

It is usually a lot more expensive to get a new customer than to sell more to existing customers.

Draw a matrix with customers on one axis and products/services on another. Is every customer buying everything you have to offer?

Customer name	Product one	Product two	Product three
Customer 1			
Customer 2			
Customer 3			
Customer 4			
Customer 5			
Customer 6			
Customer 7			
Customer 8			

Could you get repeat sales from the same customers?

Could you add extra products or services to your offering that existing customers would buy?

Before setting out to find new customers, explore ways to get more sales from existing ones:

1   List at least ten things you could you do to make more of a difference to your existing customers or clients.

2   Who else could you serve with what you do? Make a list of at least 20 people or categories of people who would benefit from what you have to offer.

3   What is your unique contribution to the work that you do? Why would anyone choose you over someone else who does something similar? This time, write down at least 50 things that make what you do and/or the way that you do it uniquely valuable in the marketplace.

What is your pricing strategy?

Selling is rarely about price and is all about perceived value, but deciding on a pricing strategy before entering into the sales process can make a big difference to your profit and helps to inform your answers if customers ask for a discount.

Discounting

As we mentioned in Chapter Three – Managing finances, discounting has a severe impact on revenue and profitability so should only be contemplated when the full financial implications are worked out and understood. On no account should sales personnel be allowed to discount prices in order to make a sale 'at any price'.

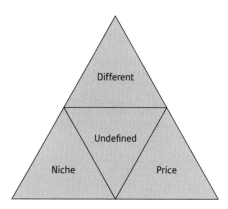

When you are offering unique or niche products or services you can charge premium prices. If you go for middle of the road you're unlikely to make much money.

▶ Different = The Only, the First, the Best …

For example, the Elite Swimming Academy hires exceptional coaches and takes only three children per class. Their results are outstanding and they charge premium prices. They always have a waiting list.

▶ Niche = We are the leaders in this sector.

For example, salsa classes for overweight men, VA services for single-parent business owners, 'fast casual' restaurants for those who want good food in the fast-food style.

▶ Price = You won't find it cheaper.

For volume businesses only, for example supermarkets, airlines.

> Which angle of the triangle is your sales proposition in?

Listening is an essential sales skill

Ask what makes a good salesperson and the unequivocal answer is 'a good listener'. Now, the listening happens online.

Where once a potential customer would ask their social group (in the pub, the gym, at the school gate or the dog-training class) for recommendations for whatever they were interested in buying, these days they use their social networks – where we can listen using simple tools.

Just like eavesdropping in the pub, you don't jump in to somebody else's conversation with a sales pitch, but hopefully, you'll already have a relationship with people who can recommend you and the potential customer will start to check you out.

> **Where once a potential customer would ask their social group for recommendations, these days they use social networks.**

They'll want to see that your social networking accounts show that you understand their needs and their values. They'll check out the way you talk to people, the way you interact with existing customers and, especially, how you handle complaints.

Meanwhile, you've added their details to your CRM system (remember, any CRM is better than none!) From there you follow them on their social networks. On Twitter you can do this without being obvious by adding them to a list rather than simply following. You can check out their LinkedIn profile and see which groups they are members of and start to interact without having to be a direct connection.

Create rapport

Every good salesperson does a lot of research before meeting a prospect but creating rapport could sometimes be a challenge before actually getting face to face. Not so now. With social networks you've probably already had several interactions and built a relationship before you get face to face.

You'll certainly know:

- ▶ not just the size but the culture of their business
- ▶ their beliefs and values
- ▶ their interests and activities

- ▶ their attitude to their customers
- ▶ what contacts you have in common
- ▶ what's happening in their world – both personal and business
- ▶ what specific problem your service or product could solve
- ▶ a LOT about their competitors.

Define your sales proposition

This is the compelling reason why people should do business with you. It should show what you offer that other people don't. Things like good value and good customer service are no more than anyone would expect so ask yourself and your customers these questions:

- ▶ What do you do that sets you apart from everyone else?
- ▶ What unique experience and background do you have that you can draw on?
- ▶ When people give you feedback, what do they say that they enjoyed or got out of the interaction?
- ▶ How can you communicate the benefits of what you do to the people that need it?
- ▶ What kind of person will want what you have to offer?
- ▶ How can you communicate that benefit in a potent way?

Features and benefits

You may hear that you should never sell features, only benefits, but this isn't always true.

There are some subtleties that are worth noting:

When to sell features

- ▶ **Low price.** If the offer is cheap enough to be seen as a 'throwaway', then you can probably sell features. Think impulse buying at the checkout counter.

▶ **Low commitment.** Something that gets used up quickly, like a stick of gum, can of coke, sandwich, or massage.

▶ **Explicit need.** You know exactly what you're looking for: a new light-bulb to replace the old broken one, or bread that's gluten free.

When to sell benefits

▶ **High price.** This is going to cost enough that careful thought is required before buying.

▶ **High commitment.** You'll be stuck with the consequences of this purchase decision for a long time, like buying a house, or joining a gym.

▶ **Vague need.** You know that you need a solution, but it isn't urgent, and you don't know exactly what – like a pension or investment plan.

Straight-up features

These are the attributes of your offer. How many units, how big in size, how long it lasts and what extras are included.

Functional outcomes

This is what they'll be able to do with the features. 'Nobody wants a drill, everybody wants a hole in the wall' – the hole in the wall is the functional outcome.

Financial outcomes

How much money will they make or save by buying this particular offer versus somebody else's? How much will they lose by not buying at all?

Experiential outcomes

What will it be like to experience the offer? Will it be fun? Exciting? You might sell tickets to a stand-up comedy show with experiential outcomes ('You'll laugh 'till you cry!').

Psychosocial benefits

What will the purchase make the buyer feel and say about themselves as a person? Think of detergent advertising – they aren't just selling the ability to clean stains out of clothes, they're selling the buyer the idea that they are a good homemaker.

What is social selling?

When social networks were hijacked and turned into media channels by marketers, the savvier of them realised that a different kind of marketing was needed. Some of them learned and some of them didn't.

The same thing is happening with sales – except that social networking is now a mature business activity and the tools that have been designed to aid the sales process are sophisticated and very effective.

Social selling should NOT be used to broadcast sales messages. While nobody joins a social network to be sold to, it doesn't mean that social networks aren't a good place to find people who want to buy from you. The thing that social selling most definitely should NOT be used for is to broadcast sales messages such as '20% off! Buy now!'

Hiring sales people

While there is a school of thought that everyone in the organisation should be a salesperson, and that the owners should definitely master this skill, there is no doubt that some people are better at it than others. Hiring a professional salesperson could be an option that overcomes other people's reluctance to sell.

Reputable tele-sales companies can fill this gap quite successfully but need to be chosen carefully. Those that employ seasoned sales professionals are a better bet than those who just cold call with a script.

Another avenue worth exploring is to find someone who sells other products and services to your target market and explore the possibility of them selling for you at the same time.

The difficulty sometimes with sales people is just that, they're sales people. If they're any good, they will have no problems in selling themselves to you and convincing you to take them on. So, how do you separate the wheat from the chaff?

1   Before the search begins, be clear on your pay structure. Will you incentivise them with a monthly bonus or a flat fee? A monthly bonus might drive them to reach their target if money is solely their driver. Could this mean, however, that they offer cut-down prices at the end of each month to help them over the line? Clear performance indicators within a set monthly salary, may be a clearer option.

2   Get a prospective salesperson to sell your product to you. If you are the product, then ask them to sell you to you, then you'll get an idea of how they will repeat this to prospective customers.

3   You wouldn't employ a salesperson to sell into the Chinese market without understanding their culture first, for fear of any reputational damage. It doesn't matter if your market is China, Leeds or the stationery industry. Above all else, ensure your sales professional understands the culture of the market you are selling in to, to make winning hearts and minds a considerably easier task.

The fear of turning down a sale

Sometimes, during the sales process, you'll get a feeling that this particular prospect could be more trouble than they're worth. Our experience of dealing with the aftermath of ignoring this type of feeling leads us to say, unequivocally, don't ignore it!

There are several myths surrounding not taking on just any old client:

Myth number one: You shouldn't turn down work because you never know when the next sale will come along.

Truth: While you're bending over backwards trying to satisfy someone who will never be satisfied you could be using that time to find more profitable customers.

Myth number two: Any work is better than no work.

Truth: If you've been beaten down on price to the point where you're not making a profit (sometimes called a loss leader!) all you're doing is using up your time and energy while you gain nothing and end up feeling bad.

Myth number three: If you do a good job, even the most awkward customer will be won over.

Truth: Most awkward customers are not interested in the quality of your work. They just want to play power games, beat you down on price, get more than you quoted for or try to avoid paying altogether. This one is a double whammy because while you're spending all your time trying to make them happy, you're not paying attention to your other perfectly good clients and they'll leave but probably won't tell you why.

What to do when your instinct is to walk away from a sale

Walk away. Just do it. Then get on the phone and follow up on some other prospects.

If the prospect jar is empty, contact your favourite clients and ask them for referrals and testimonials. Review your very best work, remind yourself how good you are then ask that client if you can use it to get you both some PR. Go networking, add to some discussions online, and shake some trees. Do anything. Just don't give yourself the grief that taking on a bad customer will bring you.

Next steps

- ▶ Start using a suitable CRM system.
- ▶ Decide on your strategy to get prospects into your sales funnel.
- ▶ Define the emotion in what you are selling.
- ▶ Fill in a customer/product matrix.
- ▶ Decide on your pricing strategy.
- ▶ Write down your unique sales proposition.
- ▶ Research the most appropriate reward package for a salesperson in your sector.

Onespacemedia

Onespacemedia started in 2008, but was re-launched in 2011 and now employs nine people. It is an award-winning digital creative business that builds large complicated websites and web application projects for organisations in many sectors, ranging from start-ups to public companies.

What skills and experience did you bring to the business? When I was very young my dad worked for Sinclair so I grew up playing with early prototypes of computers like the ZX81 and the Spectrum that he would bring home. I taught myself to program in basic from magazines like *Sinclair User* and tested games for Sinclair during the school holidays. My love for computers and technology was born. When I was 15, I did some work experience at Shandwick PR and BBH and this inspired me to want to work in the creative industries. During my teenage years I trained myself in graphic design on an Apple Mac we had at home and I earned money in my spare time on freelance jobs. My first degree was in audio engineering and I did a second degree in computer science. These early experiences gave me a rare combination of visual and technical experience. In my early thirties I was running a graphic design agency but saw that the web was becoming increasingly important. I eventually exited the graphic design business and co-founded a website agency.

What was the main difference as the business started to grow? I went from running a lifestyle graphic design business earning a decent amount of money without having to work too hard to suddenly having to pay wages, VAT, PAYE and Corporation Tax. I was working 12 hours a day for a pittance. It wasn't working out with my business partner as we had different ideas on how to run a business. I wanted to push, take risks and drive the business forward but he was more cautious. That meant that we eventually parted company and I acquired his share of the business.

When you recruit do you recruit on skills or attitude? At Onespacemedia all staff are client-facing so the team includes some great communicators. They have to rationalise the decisions they make to our clients so good writing and confident, articulate speaking are must-have skills. It goes without saying that they're also at the top of their games in their chosen disciplines.

Attitude plays a vital role. I've tried to create a working culture that allows people the creative freedom to get their tasks done in a lively environment that is more relaxed than the majority of corporate offices. This level of freedom doesn't suit everyone as it requires a high degree of responsibility to be able to work without regular instruction from a line manager.

How does that work when someone doesn't pull their weight and you have to get rid of them? We hired a designer from a big London agency and on paper he had all the right credentials. He was a lovely guy but when he started at Onespacemedia he was stunned by the speed and quality of our output. He came from a big-meeting culture and was used to producing one or two things a day, the rest of his day spent on bureaucracy. We've streamlined everything at Onespacemedia and our processes and culture allow us to churn out an incredible volume of work on any given day.

The rest of the team had started to notice the pace of his output so I had to take action. I remember the day very well. I invited him out for lunch and said 'You know it's not working, don't you?'. He had known the writing was on the wall for a while but I thought it was fair to offer him a choice – walk away then and there or have a month to try and turn it around. He chose to walk away and so I went back to the office without him.

Getting rid of an employee is a hard part of the job but as the head of a company you have to take tough decisions. It's always emotional because you've got to know people's families and friends and when someone leaves an organisation it's not easy for anyone.

How do you cope with the responsibility of making sure there is enough money to meet salaries and keep the business going? It's always stressful and I look forward to the day when cash flow isn't an issue. I've always strived to pay everyone else first. This sends out an important message to my team that they are incredibly important to the success of the business. I've never missed a payroll; I always pay suppliers on time. I've got nine people who rely on me and it's a fairly hefty payroll. We're essentially a consultancy so our ongoing revenues are growing but limited. We have to rely on a steady pipeline of work and ensure that the stages at which we are paid by clients matches our outgoings. It's a complex business and it's difficult to accurately forecast more than two or three months ahead. A lot of the time I have to go with my instincts (backed up with the experience to know that all problems are solvable). We're steadily picking up more retainer work and building a couple of digital products to improve cash flow and to help us to scale without taking on debt or releasing equity.

So you won't be looking for external investment to grow the company? The only way I would dilute our share capital is to my employees because that brings loyalty and if we ever sell the company they would get rewarded for their efforts. The only way I would take on debt funding is if I was desperate and I'd rather re-mortgage my house first before I'd take on someone that I don't know into the decision-making process. One of the most important things I learned from running a business with someone else is how equity is shared and I never want to be in a situation where I'm not the master of my own destiny – make my own decisions and take calculated risks when necessary. Fingers crossed that my approach will keep us out of the debt trap.

CHAPTER EIGHT

Managing customers

'A satisfied customer. We should have him stuffed.' (Basil Fawlty, *Fawlty Towers*).

Customer service is one of the most volatile and visible aspects of how a business is performing, in the eyes of its most important critics – its customers.

In this chapter we'll cover:

▶ the benefits of good customer service

▶ how to deliver great service

▶ how to manage customer expectations

▶ gathering feedback

▶ the customer care department.

For customers the quality of customer service determines whether to buy in the first place and then whether or not to remain a customer, irrespective of all other factors. Quality, price and all other considerations fade into insignificance when measured against poor service.

You only have to think of your own behaviour as a customer to know this is true. We've all suffered the large organisation 'take it or leave it' attitude, but small businesses have a huge advantage in that they can make customers feel really special.

Quality and price fade into insignificance when measured against poor service.

In any market or industry it costs far more to gain new customers than to retain existing customers so missing out on creating great customer relationships is like throwing money down the drain.

Benefits of good customer service

When a business gets a reputation for good customer service it has a knock-on effect in all areas of the business. Tony Hsieh, CEO of Zappos, one of the world's most successful online shoe stores, attributes the success of his enterprise to the customer service department. (He sold his company to Amazon at a valuation of $1 billion.) He says, 'Our customers did more advertising than we could pay for.' Every new person who joins the company, from cleaners to executives, spends two weeks in the customer service department.

▶ Retaining customers makes it easier to grow both indirectly and directly, for example by sustaining healthier volumes and margins, and by business expansion from word-of-mouth referrals.

▶ When customers are happy, your staff are likely to be happier and more productive. This means that you are more likely to keep your key people who in turn create good relationships with customers and keep the circle going.

▶ Happy customers mean less time spent in negotiations, arguments, bad feeling or even legal and contractual problems which are not only hugely expensive but very stressful.

▶ Having a culture of delighting and retaining customers fuels positive publicity and reputation in the media, and increasingly online. The converse applies of course, when nowadays just one disgruntled customer and a reasonable network of web friends can easily cause a significant public relations headache.

All of these benefits go straight to the bottom line. Profits are positively and directly affected by keeping customers happy, attracting new ones by word of mouth, keeping good staff, reducing stress, increasing productivity and cultivating a reputation for superb service.

Contrast the cost of delighting customers with the costs of marketing, advertising, selling, sales training, sales management, credit control and account set-up, that necessarily arise in the acquisition of new customers and it's no surprise that global management consultancy, Bain & Company, is quoted as saying that, 'It costs six to seven times more to acquire a new customer than to retain an existing one.' (**http://www.bain.com**)

Marketing has become so ubiquitous that businesses have become addicted to the hunt. We are spending billions squeezing diminishing returns from advertising and marketing, while our customers are talking to someone else.

The global spend for:

Advertising = $500 billion

CRM Systems (Contact Relationship Management) = $50 billion

Customer service = $9 billion

A business can lose anything from between 20 per cent and a staggering 80 per cent of its customers every year simply by failing to successfully manage customer relationships. In fact, the average small business will typically lose half of their customers within a three-year period.

A business can lose customers every year by failing to successfully manage customer relationships.

Imagine two businesses, one that retains 90 per cent of its customers, the other retaining 80 per cent. If both add new customers at the rate of 20 per cent per year, the first will have a 10 per cent net growth in customers per year, while the other will have none. Over seven years, the first firm will virtually double, while the second will have no real growth. Everything else being equal, that ten-point advantage in customer retention will result in a doubling of customers every seven years without doing anything else.

How good customer service is delivered

Research by the British Institute of Customer Service (ICS) identifies the following as the most important elements of service delivery according to customers:

▶ timeliness

▶ appearance

▶ courtesy

▶ quality and efficiency

▶ ease of doing business

▶ problem-solving.

Policies, systems and technology may all be part of your customer service procedure but none of these actually makes any impact on whether or not a customer feels important. Only people can do this.

The crucial constant factor in great customer relationships is the human element. People respond to other people better than they do to machines and pre-determined processes.

The key skills involved are:

1   empathy

2   communication – verbal, non-verbal and written

3   handling stress

4   active listening

5   team-working

6   problem-solving and complaints-handling

7   product and organisation knowledge

8   commitment to the aims and values of the business.

To improve your customer service, answer these questions:

▶   What does great service look like and feel like?

▶   What kind of first impression does your business give?

▶   What would be the best and worst experience of dealing with your business?

▶   What is the responsibility of everyone in your business for customer service?

▶   Stepping into your customers' shoes, how do you feel about your business?

▶   What things are most likely to cause disappointment?

▶   What actions will you take that could turn disappointment into delight?

▶   In what way could you add value and exceed customer expectations?

Good practice

A young boy wanted to buy his parents a thank you gift for taking him to Disneyland. He spent the last of his pocket money on salt and pepper pots with Mickey Mouse ears from the gift shop. As he ran back to give the gift to his parents he tripped and dropped the bag, shattering the ceramic pots. A passing Disney employee helped to pick them up and suggested he take them back to the shop. The boy was sceptical as he had been the one to drop them but, with a bit of urging, went back to the store. The response from the assistant at the till was unequivocal. He peered into the bag and said, 'I'm so sorry. I didn't wrap them well enough' and promptly replaced them.

The boy, Randy Pausch, his sister and their parents reckon that as a result of that small action they spent over $100,000 with the Disney brand over the years. Furthermore, Randy went on to become a scientist and professor who gave lectures all over the world and told that story over and over to thousands of people.

The effect of reciprocity

Human beings like to return favours, pay back debts and treat others as they treat us. We're uncomfortable with feeling indebted to others. Although this has been the case for years, the impact of social media has increased this further with customer service now being even more about reciprocity. When you do something amazing for a customer it produces a powerful psychological state of deep-seated motivation and they feel they have to do something amazing back – like share with the world how wonderful you are.

Managing customer expectations

Once again we refer back to Chapter One – Managing the business, and the importance of clearly stating the purpose of your business and your values. These are essential tools in managing customer expectations.

Do you have clear terms and conditions? Do they give clear specifications about how you work, what you expect from your client and what they can expect from you? If not that's easily sorted. Less easy is how you handle 'scope creep' – the extras that a client asks you to do without charging – but once you've got that sorted in your head and know how to value your work, it is much easier to deal with – before it becomes an issue.

Customer feedback

We all love to get positive feedback and it is such a powerful indicator of future satisfaction that the reputations of many businesses depend on it. Sellers on eBay and re-sellers on Amazon both rely on their feedback ratings to attract more business.

However, it's not enough to know that we're doing it right. Remember that most dissatisfied customers will simply walk away without telling us if something is wrong, so we need to constantly ask how they're feeling to help us to get better.

It's imperative that every customer should have a platform to tell you their thoughts, whether positive or not, and the easier it is for them to respond, the more likely they are to do so. Timing is also key and it's best to collect customer feedback within a week of their transaction, rather than a month or longer.

It's imperative that every customer should have a platform to tell you their thoughts.

To encourage feedback, try offering an incentive like an entry in a prize draw for a completed feedback form. The more responses you receive, the better your data will be.

Ways to get feedback

Email

The key to this is to ask the right question. A simple two-question process is a good example of how to approach this:

1   Would you recommend us to a friend?

2   Why?

Survey

A great source of customer data for many businesses is surveys. Using a free service such as Survey Monkey makes this simple, but care needs to go into formatting the questions. It is easy to lead people into giving the answers you'd like to see so make sure the wording is absolutely neutral. If you are expecting a large number of responses, the data should be easy to analyse, so tick boxes rather than written responses may be the best option but won't give the same depth of insight.

Social media

Make it a habit to ask customers which social networks they use and that they know they can contact you there. Set up alerts for your company name to see what customers may be saying about you indirectly and be sure to respond. There is more on this topic in Chapter Four – Managing social media.

Finally, be sure to follow up on your responses where possible, even if that is a simple 'thank you'. Make your customer feel that their thoughts have been taken on board, especially if you're going to ask them again after their next purchase.

Most of our revenue comes from existing customers

Adobe Digital Index analysed 33 billion visits to websites in Europe and the United States from April 2011 to June 2012. They found that 92 per cent was new visitor traffic and these visitors produced 59 per cent of revenue. Visits by existing customers were just 8 per cent of traffic, but income from existing customers was 41 per cent of total revenue.

The amount of money and effort involved in attracting new visits to a website to produce a relatively small difference in revenue compared to the amount generated by existing customers makes no sense at all. Looking after existing customers clearly pays off and brings repeat revenue for little additional expense.

So, why is customer service such a great revenue generator? Research from well-respected organisations has found ten more reasons:

1   Price is NOT the main reason for customer loss; it is actually due to the overall poor quality of customer service.

2   The probability of selling to an existing customer is three to ten times more likely than selling to a new prospect.

3   For every customer complaint there are 26 other unhappy customers who have remained silent.

4   96 per cent of unhappy customers don't complain; however, 91 per cent of those will simply leave and never come back.

5   Since the advent of Facebook, Twitter, Instagram and the rest, a dissatisfied consumer will now tell several thousand people of their experience.

6   Equally, happy customers who get their issue resolved, especially if it happens on social media, also tell thousands of people.

7   55 per cent of customers would pay extra to guarantee better service.

8   It takes 12 positive experiences to make up for one unresolved negative experience.

9   A 5 per cent reduction in the customer defection rate can increase profits by 5–95 per cent.

10   It costs six to seven times more to acquire a new customer than to retain an existing one.

Good practice

Here are some of examples of customer service that this author (Ed Goodman) has experienced:

Too often, customer service is thought of solely as a reaction to a customer complaint or a measured response to a piece of feedback. Very often customers don't complain, they just don't come back.

Last summer I visited a sports shop to buy a pair of trainers. When I found the ones I liked, I handed them to the shop assistant and asked for them in my size. After a few minutes, she returned and handed me the shoes

---

back saying, 'We don't have them in stock I'm afraid.' Instead of offering an alternative pair or finding out more about what I was after, she simply walked away. So I walked out and have never been back. I'm not alone here. Around 90 per cent of UK shoppers walk away without buying something if they get bad customer service. How can anyone react to customer emotions that they never get to hear them?

This works both ways though. Checking in to a flight at Vienna Airport returning to the UK via Germany the ground crew told me that because the flight was taking off late they would need to rush me off the plane at Berlin and get me quickly to my connecting flight. On arrival, nothing happened and I missed my flight. I was tired and angry that I was promised an action that never happened. Once I got to the Air Berlin customer service desk I had mentally prepared my words to express how unhappy I was, only to be met by:

'Before you say anything Mr Goodman, you've missed your flight to the UK, there are no more this evening and there is nothing I can do about that. However, I have a taxi outside waiting to take you to a hotel which I've booked you into. You will also receive a meal, and tomorrow morning you will be picked up at 5.30 to bring you back here where you're booked on the first flight home. Any questions?'

… er, no!!

Not all customers are worth keeping

If you have a client or customer who makes you feel sick every time you hear them on the phone, then it's probably time to let them go. The call could probably be bringing a deadline forward, changing the scope of the project, making unreasonable demands or haggling over an invoice. Either way, it's impossible to do good work under these circumstances and even if good work gets done, it doesn't get recognised.

If you do good work (and a bad client can cause you to doubt this, but that's another story) you deserve praise and satisfaction as well as money for your work.

Picture this scenario; you have a great client and a client from hell. Which one do you spend most time thinking about, most time trying to please, most time worrying what they think of you? You guessed it, the wrong one, that's who! This is the equivalent of putting your picnic blanket next to a cow pat when you could put it next to patch of daisies!

The time you spend trying to appease a hopeless cause could be spent finding more good clients.

The double bind is that while you spend so much time on the annoying client your good clients could feel neglected. At worst, this could result in your good clients looking elsewhere for the service that you're supposed to be providing. The time you spend trying to appease a hopeless cause could be spent finding more good clients or giving better service to the ones you really want to keep.

If you have a client that takes up too much head space, makes you feel sick and is stopping you from getting on with the work you love to do, the first step is to tell them that you have a problem with them and invoke your T&Cs. If that doesn't work there's only one solution …

Sack them.

Walk away from them.

Don't look back.

Spend the time you have available finding clients who love you.

Customer care

Zappos, mentioned earlier in this chapter, has become a watchword for customer care. The online shoe retailer stocks 90,000 styles and more than 500 brands and has 500 employees in a call centre in Las Vegas who have all received seven weeks of training on how to make customers happy. The company has been called both 'insane' and 'fanatical' for the way it will do anything to please its customers. The stories are legendary, and are a key part of its brand. Here are some fantastic examples of their 'insane' service levels:

▶ Zappos sent flowers to a woman who ordered six different pairs of shoes because her feet were damaged by harsh medical treatments.

▶ A customer service rep physically went to a rival shoe store to get a specific pair of shoes for a customer and personally delivered them to the hotel she was staying because Zappos had run out of stock.

▶ A best man who had arrived at a wedding shoeless phoned to ask if he could get a pair of shoes delivered overnight. Zappos sent them free. Not just free delivery, free shoes.

Everyone in the company – without exception, from cleaners to executives – is trained for four weeks in customer service and encouraged to use their own social networking accounts to engage with customers and help solve their problems in their own time as well as while they are at work.

Many businesses say they are 'customer-centric' while treating their staff like second-class citizens and wonder why it is difficult to get staff to treat their customers well. At Zappos and most other businesses that care about their customers, it's not just their staff that are treated well (free health insurance, free meals, good pay and conditions), this ethos extends to suppliers and all stakeholders.

The company's extranet lets vendors see which shoes are selling and how profitably, making it less likely that they'll run out of popular lines. Zappos even holds a vendor appreciation party before the big industry trade show each year. And yes, the call centre staff are all invited. No wonder there's a big queue of people wanting to work for them.

And it pays off.

Good practice

A few years ago, if you wanted an accounts package for your small business, there wasn't much to choose from. Two major players dominated the market and they didn't suit many customers. A group of friends built a product called Freeagent that perfectly fitted their needs and, in 2013, Freeagent topped Deloitte's list of fastest growing technology firms. The product was built by the people who were its first customers and customer feedback continues to be a major part of its development. This is how they did it:

▶

It sounds unlikely that a hugely successful accounts package was built by an ex-RAF Harrier pilot, a condensed matter physicist, and a scuba diver, but that's exactly what happened! Ed Molyneux, Roan Lavery and Olly Headey were all freelancers looking for a simple online solution to manage their finances, and couldn't find one, so they decided to build their own.

They wanted a straightforward tool to facilitate collaboration with their accountants in a way that existing desktop software or spreadsheets could not. They shared the initial product with friends in the freelancer space, found that their friends were not only using it but also recommending it on, and they realised that they had a potentially saleable and scalable product on their hands.

Customer service comes from a team of accountants and bookkeepers, and feedback is collected as part of the email and phone support service and there is also a publicly accessible customer forum, monitored by both the support team and product development team, where anyone is welcome to make suggestions for how the product might be improved. Customers are also encouraged to vote for changes they would like to see.

The 90-day rule

There used to be a rule that you should contact all of your customers and prospects at the very least every 90 days. These days, this is far too long. Use social media channels, newsletters and blogs to give them useful information, keep your name in front of them at least once a month and let them know that you value them.

Next steps

Customer service is intrinsic in everything a business does. Here are three simple tips to focus on:

1   **Start right now**. The next person who calls you or walks through your door could become a customer. Treat them with the respect that your existing customers would expect. How they feel will affect their buying decision and determine how they speak about you. Even if they don't buy from you, there is every chance that they know someone who is looking for what you offer.

2   **Ask your customers**. We're often afraid of asking because we're unsure of the response. But why? What's the worst that can happen? If they hate you and never plan to buy from you again, find out why. If you're not sure what to ask, these two simple questions are enough:

   ▶   Would you recommend me/us to a friend?

   ▶   Why?

3   **Give your customers a platform.** If your customers' emotions have been pushed to one end of the spectrum or another, good or bad, they will talk about you. Therefore, it's best to know what they're saying. Have a page on your website or encourage them to use your social media feeds, but give them a chance to say how wonderful you are or what you can do better.

As Walt Disney famously said, 'Whatever you do, do it well. Do it so well that when people see you do it they will want to come back and see you do it again and they will want to bring others and show them how well you do what you do'.

The Elite Swimming Academy

Ed Williams is the Managing Director of The Elite Swimming Academy. He started the business in 2006 when he was just 20 years old and now employs 18 swimming teachers and four admin assistants. They teach over 1,000 people a week and have an annual turnover of £600,000.

What made you decide to start your business? It was accidental, it really started as a hobby business just to keep some money coming in when my previous boss couldn't afford to keep me on and was never intended to be a long time career. Up until a couple of years ago, my mother would often ask when I was going to get a proper job!

What experience did you bring to your business? I am dyslexic, not at all academic and swimming is the only thing I've ever been really good at. I was one of the youngest people in history to swim the English Channel when I was just 19 and so swimming was the only skill I brought to the business. I started with just a handful of private clients and got good results so I just kept going.

How did you decide on your business model? Leisure centres have about 20 kids in a class and charge about £3 per lesson. We have three kids in a class and charge £17 a lesson. It quickly became clear that there was a niche for high-quality swimming tuition. We were charging a premium price and always had a waiting list. We get the same profit but much higher quality tuition so much better results and that is why we always have a waiting list.

Did you do a market analysis to arrive at your pricing structure? No, the company I used to work for had a similar business model but I took it and made it better. We created more actual and perceived value. We weren't the first in this market and we won't be the last but we always strive to be the best. We now guarantee our results and we never fail to deliver.

Did you have any investment to get the business started? No, we did everything on a shoe-string. I knocked up a logo and a simple website and paid for the pool hire after the customer paid us. The success of this business has enabled me to invest in other businesses and I now have some property lets and holiday homes.

Do you still work full time in the business? I'm still the Managing Director but my goal was always to have a lifestyle business and not to work seven days a week. About three years ago I took myself out of the business 100 per cent and did a lot of travelling and generally had a good time. Eventually I got bored and noticed that the quality of our service was slipping so I came back to do three half days a week and now I spend time training to do extreme swimming challenges which allows me to raise a lot of money for charity and also gets me lots of PR.

What are your most successful marketing tactics? My most successful marketing tactic has been to use my Channel swim to inspire children. I offer to go into the school of children who are our customers to take an assembly about my Channel swims and tell them stories of dodging jellyfish and giant ships! The children are all captivated and inspired and we always get lots of bookings after these talks. This approach costs me nothing and is by far the most powerful.

What are the biggest challenges you've had to deal with? My biggest challenge was managing people. I was much younger than a lot of the people I employed and found it difficult to tell people what to do and especially to discipline them. I take the same approach to overcoming business problems as I do to overcoming problems in people learning to swim. I recognise them, acknowledge them, discuss them, strip them down and put processes in place to make sure the same things don't keep happening again.

Where have you found the most support? When we were just 20-year-olds my fiancée kept me on the right track and now that we're married she is a co-director of the business and still my biggest supporter. I am a big picture person and she would always analyse and fill in the details and make sure things would work. We've branched out into other projects like underwater photography and swim shops and discovered that these didn't make any money so we now run them as outsourced or affiliate services and make more money doing very little work.

What is your vision for the future? This is a topic of constant debate in our household! We could go for world domination and grow to a multi-million pound business but this would involve a lot of time and it isn't really why we started the business. We have a growing family and want to spend time having a great lifestyle. If we were to sell the business we'd look for a price of around £5 milion but we're still very young so we're not sure we want to go down that route just yet. For the time being we're continuing as we are and considering putting a Managing Director in place to manage the day-to-day activities.

What advice would you give to someone starting out in business? Don't try to please everyone! On the rare occasion that a customer is upset it upsets me on a visceral level. I always call them personally and that usually clears everything up because people don't expect it but that desire for perfection is a problem. Perfection isn't a bad thing to strive for but it's not always achievable and if you become obsessed by it as I was, it can cause a lot of stress for everyone around you.

What tips would you give to anyone going from starting out to growing a business? In order to grow a business you have to take yourself out of it in terms of doing the work. I know this is what a lot of people struggle with. When I hired my first teachers I used to say to my wife, every night, this is never going to work, they're never going to do as good a job as me, the customers want me. Of course it turned out they were doing an even better job than me. When you give up 100 per cent control you need to have faith and trust in other people and if you've chosen them well and have the right systems in place, it will still flow nicely. Otherwise you're just swapping your time for money and you can't grow a business that way. There's a ceiling point then and you don't have enough hours in the day, whereas the more people you take on and you're charging for their time the future is endless.

9

CHAPTER NINE

Managing people

One of the things that stops businesses from growing is when a business owner tries to do everything themselves in the belief that no one would do the job as well as they can. There is also an emotional attachment of 'not letting go'.

In this chapter we'll look at:

▶ letting go

▶ recruiting for skills and attitudes

▶ organisation style

▶ trust, responsibility and time management

▶ employment and the law

▶ how to build a perfectly formed small team and thrive.

If you don't yet employ other people, you will need to consider outsourcing or directly employing people or a combination of both, as the business grows.

This is an area that often causes business owners the most anxiety and frustration for a number of reasons. For some it is about finding the right people, for others it is the time and effort involved in training and managing others and for some, the whole area of employment legislation feels very threatening.

To continue to grow your business, you need to learn to delegate and manage properly, giving up day-to-day control of every detail. It's all too easy to stifle creativity and motivation with excessive interference.

To continue to grow your business, you need to learn to delegate and manage.

Expert opinion Neil Bharadwa, Cambridge Fruit Company

I set up the Cambridge Fruit Company on my own nine years ago. For the best part of eight years and ten months I've just had my head down in the business and spent way too much time either in the trenches or putting out the fires. This meant I started to feel negatively about my business that I had been so passionate about. The spark had been lost. I've only grown organically and added staff to suit but recently I took a bigger jump and actually invested in staff to replace me.

I advertised the positions for free on Gumtree and interviewed the most likely candidates. The most important thing for me was their attitude to hard work. I deduced this from interviews but far more importantly – calling up their previous employers.

It hasn't been long, but since then I've had so much more time to focus on the things I enjoy and I'm utilising my skills on what I'm best at – sales and marketing. I've added four new customers in the last few weeks alone. What I've learned is that NOT recruiting staff to do the 'easy' stuff is a false economy. It won't save you any money – it'll cost you more in the long term. I know it's a cliché but I've now got so much more time to work ON my business instead of IN my business.

Following Neil Bharadwa's example, answer the following questions:

▶ What extra skills are you likely to need?

▶ What parts of the business might other people do better than you?

▶ Do you favour outsourcing or employing the people you need?

▶ Does your current pricing structure support paying other people?

▶ If you already outsource or employ people take some time to make an honest assessment of the service you are getting.

▶ Is it adequate for your needs? Are you delighted or disappointed with the people you pay?

▶ What changes, if any, do you need to make?

Skills and attitude

One of the most important features of any successful business is a trusting, professional relationship between the employer and staff. Getting the right people is not just about having the right skills. Personality and motivation are important in making sure people fit into a team. Many business owners prefer to 'recruit for attitude and train for skills', but of course this all depends on the job and how easy it is to train the right person. One thing is certain: having someone with the right skills who doesn't fit the company culture or values will be extremely disruptive and may cause other valued members of staff to leave.

> **Personality and motivation are important in making sure people fit into a team.**

There are various tools that can be used to assess personality and motivation and others that ensure you have a balanced team. Most of these need to be delivered by a trained practitioner and not all are very reliable so this option needs to be handled with caution.

Interviews are the cheapest but often the least reliable method of employing people. You will need to think about the following:

▶ What key skills do you need to expand the business?

▶ Are you clear on the attitudes and values you expect people to have?

▶ How do you propose to discover if applicants will be a good fit with your business?

How to attract the right people

Pay and conditions of work are obviously important, but they don't outweigh other factors. Most people put job satisfaction and relationships with the people they work with above all other factors.

Google has been named the world's best company to work for five times in a row (**www.fortune.com**). You may think that this is easy when they have plenty of resources, but plenty of very profitable companies don't get it right.

In the *Sunday Times* 'Best Small Companies to Work For' list the nominees are marked on the following categories:

▶ **Leadership.** How employees feel about the head of the company and its senior managers.

▶ **Wellbeing.** How staff members feel about the stress, pressure and the balance between their work and home duties.

▶ **Giving something back.** How much companies are thought by their staff to put back into society generally and the local community.

▶ **Personal growth.** To what extent staff members feel they are stretched and challenged by their job.

▶ **My manager.** How staff members feel towards their immediate boss and day-to-day managers.

▶ **My company.** Feelings about the company people work for as opposed to the people they work with.

▶ **My team.** How staff members feel about their immediate colleagues.

▶ **Fair deal.** How happy the workforce is with their pay and benefits.

> If employees were to mark your company on these criteria, how do you think you'd fare?

Recruitment process

1 Check the latest employment laws. These change regularly so, if in doubt, its best to ask a professional Human Resources consultant.

2 List the skills and attitudes you need your ideal candidate to have. Their values need to match those of your business.

3 Write a job description that is based on results and outcomes rather than processes.

4 Design practical tests and interview questions that you will use for all candidates that will reveal both skills and attitudes. 'Tell me about a time when ...' is a good way to find out about past behaviour and a good way to predict future behaviour.

5 Craft an advertisement that is clear about what the person needs to be able to do. You must ensure your advertisement and appointment is fair and legal. Check with your HR consultant to make sure your selection

process does not inadvertently discriminate on grounds of gender, age, ethnicity or disability.

6 Do a phone interview with likely candidates. Ask everyone the same questions and record their answers.

7 Make your shortlist and invite people for a face-to-face interview.

8 Be clear about contract terms. Make sure that the person is making an informed choice and there are no nasty surprises later. Find out what the person's expectations of the job are and be honest if these are not really compatible with yours. It is important that the person has enough information to make a decision if you make them an offer.

9 We all make assumptions and we all have prejudices. When it comes to making appointments you need to be aware of these and make a conscious decision to override them. If getting along well as part of the team is important, how can you break this down into specific behaviour? Is it really important that the person likes cricket and beer or is it actually that they share information and ideas, help others and can accept criticism?

10 Ask for and check references, qualifications, driving licence if appropriate, and any other material that may prove to be important in the future. If in doubt, don't appoint.

11 Support them when they arrive. Having got your appointment right, make sure that the new person's arrival and induction gets off to a good start. Make sure physical space and resources have been prepared so they are not floundering without a computer or email address. Take sufficient time to ensure that your new person understands what they are to achieve and how to go about this. Hand over the relevant information and access to systems.

12 Always have a probationary period. Set clear expectations for this and meet regularly to discuss whether these are being met.

Organisation style

Before employing other people you need to decide what style of organisation you want to run. The traditional top-down, command and control hierarchy may suit you or you may decide that a flatter, more democratic organisation has advantages. A lot will depend on your personal style but also on the type of business and the nature of the people you employ. Some people like autonomy and some like to be managed so it's harder to change once you have people in place. We touched on this briefly in Chapter Two – Managing growth.

Many business owners find the hardest part of growing a business is not knowing the names of all the people they employ.

Many business owners find the hardest part of growing a business is when they get to the point of not knowing the names of all the people they employ.

Advice on traditional management styles is plentiful and can be found in thousands of books, blogs, articles and training programmes.

The most famous example of democratising a workplace is SemcoSA, a Brazilian company best known for its radical form of industrial democracy and corporate re-engineering. Its 30-year experiment is detailed in a book called *Maverick* written by Ricardo Semler the CEO and majority owner (Random House Business, 2001).

Valve, a video game company with a staff of 300 and an estimated value of £2.4 billion, is one of a small number of firms to adopt a 'flat', manager-less structure. Business teams are formed and reformed based on projects that need completing, and decisions are made democratically – 'the best idea wins, no matter who it comes from' is a favourite saying of the CEO.

Morning Star, a tomato-processing firm, operates with employees who draw up their own personal mission statements describing how they will use their skills to meet the firm's targets. The parameters and budgets of an individual's plan are negotiated with peers, as is compensation. The result, as demonstrated in Semco (see above), is that employees end up taking on a far higher level of responsibility for their work, with the firm boasting double-digit growth rates compared to one per cent for the wider market.

Wordpress, one of the world's most popular blogging platforms whose customers include CNN, eBay, Sony, Reuters and General Motors is run by a small company called Automattic, Inc. The company has approximately 250 employees who work from wherever they choose in any location in the world and communicate with each other on projects via an intranet that is open to anyone in the company to see and comment on.

Other examples of democratised businesses are celebrated every year in the World Blu list (**http://worldblu.com/**). These include every type of business from manufacturing to transport services, from cloud-based technology to education.

Trust, responsibility and time management

As soon as you employ other people, you need to give them responsibility for doing their job which means that you need to trust them. This can sometimes be difficult for business owners who have been used to doing everything themselves.

As soon as you employ other people, you need to give them responsibility and trust them.

If you appoint managers you have to resist the temptation to circumvent them by going directly to your employees, or making decisions without involving your new management team. You can no longer behave as the founder who deals with all issues and has a direct line to every employee in the company. If you do, you run the risk of losing your managers and confusing your staff.

Your attitudes to customers and other members of staff are likely to be picked up and imitated by your employees so your leadership style is very important. Similarly, your time management is likely to set the tone for the company so if you are late in delivering services or over-promise and under-deliver your staff members are likely to do the same.

> Are you comfortable managing other people and helping them to develop? Are there areas you need help with?

Employment and the law

It can sometimes seem that employment law is designed to put off any small business from employing people. The good news is that there are lots of independent Human Resources advisors who specialise in helping small businesses to be good employers and keep on the right side of the law.

If you choose to employ people, a contract of employment is a legal requirement. A job description combined with a simple staff handbook will encompass all aspects of your staff policies and procedures and should give every employee sufficient guidelines for what is expected of them and what they can expect in return.

If you choose to outsource you may need a contract to ensure continuity and confidentiality.

What are the main elements of an employee handbook or a contract for outsourcing your business?

This is the entire wording of the employee handbook of Nordstrom – a leading fashion specialty retailer based in the US. Founded in 1901 as a shoe store in Seattle, the company now operates stores throughout the US and in Canada:

EMPLOYEE HANDBOOK

Our number one goal is to provide outstanding customer service. Set both your personal and professional goals high. We have great confidence in your ability to achieve them, so our employee handbook is very simple. We have only one rule...

NORDSTROM

OUR ONE RULE
Use good judgment in all situations.

Please feel free to ask your department manager, store manager or Human Resources any questions at any time.

You decide how much more you want, in the knowledge that as soon as you get lawyers involved there is a vested interest in making things as complicated as possible.

Expert opinion Judith Elliott, Director at el:consulting and el:talking, and a specialist in people management

How to build a perfectly formed team and thrive

The best managers construct a framework of actions around the main focus of getting the job done, which increases the efficiency, decreases stress and is ultimately more rewarding for all concerned.

Management is complex job because we have tasks to perform, results to deliver, plus we have to juggle all our skills to get our people firing on all

▶

cylinders. The truly successful managers are the ones who have a set of processes in place to make that happen; a framework or 'scaffolding' that allows them to easily and seamlessly do all those management things like big picture planning, delegating, motivating and so on.

Just because you are in a small business doesn't mean you don't need scaffolding; you just need less of it. Remember you can build some and then take part down. Try it out and if it's not right, change the shape.

A handful of simple mechanisms or actions impact on the effectiveness of any organisation because they literally enable and encourage managers to use all the basic leadership skills.

The top five pieces of scaffolding are:

1   **Context.** Set a clear vision for where your business is heading and then communicate that to employees. A clear purpose – what are we here for? What sort of behaviour will get us there? This all sets the context and the tone. Think: do we want to be an Aldi or a Waitrose or a niche food retailer? High end, fast turnover, experts? Rapid growth or steady as she goes?

    Your people need to know this so that they can be the people you want them to be. They need to understand the ambition or the level of service that your business must give to succeed, so knowing the direction and position in the market gives them clarity.

    This also means that you recruit the right people in the first place; square pegs in round holes are never a good idea.

2   **The job description**. Usually a long-winded document full of vacuous statements and woolly verbs, usually written in a hurry when recruiting and then put in a filing cabinet never to see the light of day again, until ten years down the line when you realise that the person you recruited has just turned the job into the one they want it to be, and not the one you had in mind.

    If you write a good, concise job description that actually specifies outcomes for the job role you have, then you've got the basis for a robust interview (looking for evidence to meet those outcomes) and also a live document to manage and assess performance.

3   **A communication framework**. We all tend to believe that very small teams don't need meetings or formal communications but this is valid only to a point. If you can all fit in one minibus to go to the pub, most useful stuff will get communicated somehow, but people need regular messages and in different formats for different reasons. For example, if you only communicate informally about tasks then you may be missing the opportunity to talk about the big picture; the context, the vision, the overall behaviour required.

So to get the right communication framework you will need the right mix of meetings, one-to-ones, and big picture days. It's worth sitting down and doing a communication plan – just a chart – that details which topics you'll talk about in which format.

4   **Performance reviews.** Every one of us deserves to have our boss's undivided attention at least once a year; a chance to reflect on our performance, our aspirations, maybe even get some good quality praise. Chances are you're good at the informal expressions of appreciation, but are you any good at specifying exactly what they did right? Performance management is not complicated, you just have to be doing it all the time, and start from the beginning.

5   **Successful people management**

▶   **Clarity**. People need to know exactly what is expected of them; not to be told *what* to do or necessarily *how* to do it, but what the *results* should be (the outcomes). They could have a better way of doing things than you, so take care to be clear on the results you want, and help them work out how to achieve it if they need help, but ultimately agree outcomes. This is where a good job description is a useful tool and also the skill of how to delegate; agree outcomes, not a 'to do' list. With clarity comes transparency. I was told as a young manager that I needed to feel that I was managing in a goldfish bowl so the justification for every decision was obvious and clear. This means that you have to explain your thinking.

▶   **Integrity**. People can see right through manipulation and waffle. You need to be seen as trustworthy and it's the little things that you do that build up to the whole integrity image. For example, never talk about one person in the team to someone else, never expose confidences, never make promises you can't keep, treat people with respect. And do it consistently ... oh and be consistent.

▶ **Feedback**. The big one so let's cut to the chase here. Feedback is the wrong word. Always start with a question; never, ever, go straight into feedback. Use the wide frame approach instead, e.g. 'I thought we had decided the report would be with me by Friday; was there a problem?'. This recognises a problem but allows the employee the opportunity to put their case first. You listen, maybe ask another question and decide what next. If they have obviously learned from their mistake you don't need to be hard on them at all. If this is actually someone else's mistake you won't have egg on your face. People will take feedback if they feel that the feedback process is fair. By asking them first you are showing the highest level of fairness.

▶ **Catch them doing something right**. This originates with management guru Tom Peters. Don't spend all your time telling people off. In fact if you have to do that something is very wrong, and usually it will be your fault. People thrive on praise and wilt under criticism so make your secret weapon an active policy of finding something to praise.

Next steps

The following is a set of actions or processes you put in place to engage employees in what you are trying to achieve. If one of the statements doesn't apply to your business, leave it blank or cross it out.

Scoring

2 = The whole organisation understands and is engaged with this process.

1 = A bit hit and miss – there is more work to do in this area.

0 = Nowhere near it – I have to start planning how to achieve this.

Business strategy	Score
We have clearly defined objectives covering the key areas of our business, e.g. people, sales, profit.	
These objectives are reviewed at least monthly as part of my business planning.	
It is clear to everyone how individual strategies connect with the overall business strategy.	
The overall business strategy is jargon free and easily understandable by anyone inside or outside the business.	
Business objectives are all SMART (Specific, Measurable, Achievable, Realistic, Time-bound).	
Operational plans	
We have an achievable, stretching but realistic, plan suitable for our type of business.	
Key team members report to me on progress on a regular (pre-set) basis.	
Information flow	
All messages go out from me using the appropriate channel, e.g. internal before external, managers before employees.	
My team tells me everything I need to know without being asked all the time.	
We have good two-way communication in the organisation.	
I communicate with the board and any stakeholders effectively.	
We keep systems simple and effective.	

▶

Knowledge management	Score
As an organisation we look at the results we want to achieve and then work out what knowledge we need to achieve those results.	
We share knowledge effectively.	
I connect with key people in the business on a regular basis.	
Managing performance	
Every individual in my organisation knows exactly what is expected of them.	
Every individual in my organisation receives the appropriate development to achieve their objectives.	
I give praise when it is due.	
I give constructive feedback to the team and individuals.	
I provide resources and support for people to do their jobs effectively.	
I set performance standards which will enable us all to achieve our objectives.	
People are paid the right salary to fit with market rate and their effort.	
We have the right amount and mix of meetings to do our jobs well.	
I can reward individuals who make extra special efforts.	
People who underperform are helped to achieve an acceptable performance.	
Team members connect with the right people outside the business on a regular and effective basis.	
The team feeds back constructive reports on progress and big picture issues	

Breckland Orchard

Claire Martinsen is the Managing Director of Breckland Orchard. She manufactures and distributes her own brand of gently carbonated soft drinks known to its fans as Posh Pop. The range is sold to independent outlets: coffee shops, farm shops and gastropubs across the UK as well as five overseas markets and has been operating since March 2009.

How long did it take from idea to actually producing/delivering a product?
I had the idea for a few months, whilst I was off on maternity leave with my second child. I'd been juggling a job in a large company, which entailed a very long commute to work, and numerous early starts and late nights. I came to realise that with two children that juggle was going to be impossible to maintain.

I resigned my job in October 2008, and my first bottle came off the production line in February 2009, so it was a relatively quick process. I was fortunate that having worked in a manufacturing/branded business I knew some of the elements that would be required to start production, but I was also fortunate to meet some great people at the start who helped me get up and running.

How was the business funded at the start? I was self-funded and continue to be so … I have a very supportive husband who shares my risk-taking philosophy!

What experience did you bring to the business? I have a degree in marketing and then spent 15 years in a variety of sales/account management roles for large companies. I think that gave me a background of discipline especially as far as plans, forecasts and general business experience. But at the same time I knew absolutely nothing about soft drinks apart from drinking them, so that's been a steep learning curve.

Even with that commercial background, I still made a number of errors – especially in the early days. My first strap line of 'local soft drinks that sparkle' became redundant 12 weeks after launch when I started selling out with the East of England – I perhaps should have predicted that!

What have been your most successful marketing tactics? I embraced social media very early on, and it's worked brilliantly for me along the way. I didn't have the funds to do a big marketing campaign, so social media allows small businesses like mine to shout with far more clout than using other types of marketing. In some ways it allows big and smaller companies to play on a level playing ground. I do all the social media myself and it gives a very authentic and natural feel to the business, as well as being able to interact directly with the customers of my drinks!

What has been your biggest business challenge? Managing growth and cash is always a challenge, especially in a manufacturing business where stocks need to be built up around key trading times. In some ways that's become more important the older the company becomes and where the need to have great supply gets critical.

I took the decision relatively early into starting the business not to supply supermarkets and to focus instead on coffee shops, farm shops and delicatessens. The soft drinks market is incredibly competitive and it made sense to select just a part of it rather than trying to focus on everything. It means I can be clear about who my potential customers are, and therefore be more effective with my marketing. When I look back over the past five years, I can spot that all my lightbulb moments have been when I've honed what I'm doing and been both narrower and clearer about what Breckland Orchard stands for.

I know that it's oft quoted that you should be more niche to grow more and having done it, and deliberately not tried to satisfy too many markets, I can honestly say it helps to know what you stand for (and more importantly what you don't stand for!).

How did you cope with having to manage the business instead of working in it? I have a strong plan which is the backbone of the business and reminds me of what's important. All those years writing annual plans/sales plans/marketing plans/launch plans prior to starting Breckland Orchard have stood me in good stead, and just the act of writing and then measuring is helpful.

What other challenges did you have? I started the business with a baby and a two-year-old in tow, and even though they are now older, it's been 'interesting' juggling it all. At times Breckland Orchard felt like a third child, but in truth I wouldn't have had it any other way.

Who have you got support from? Before I started, I thought running my own business would be a lonely experience, but it's been anything but. I've got great friends, who are in business locally, friends within the food/drink sector and also some great mentors. I have a tendency to be very self-critical, and they definitely keep me grounded and remind me what a great brand I've built from scratch.

What is the most useful piece of advice you had when you started? Go with your gut instinct. If it doesn't feel right then don't go with it. Good advice, as small businesses don't have the time to spend lots of time evaluating. I changed my accountant after six months, despite having taken time choosing them in the first place prior to starting up. It just didn't feel right, and changing to my new accountants was one of the best things I ever did.

What tip would you offer someone who is making the transition from starting out to growing their business? Don't be afraid to make mistakes – nothing ventured, nothing gained. It's a bit like rock climbing, when you are in the early years, falling off is low-risk as you are quite near the bottom. Make mistakes, and take risks whilst you are small, nimble and growing – those risks are harder to take when you are bigger! Also, I have a mix of full-time employees, part-time employees and lots of freelancers (e.g. virtual PA's/bookkeepers) who work for me on a regular basis. Freelancers are a great way for a growing business to get the regular input of true experts in their field but for the hours I need them. It works brilliantly and I'm a huge advocate of growing and developing in this way. You can increase hours as and when the business requires it.

10

Managing your exit

In the thrill of launching and growing a business it can sometimes be hard to imagine how it will all end. Some business owners get quite cross when asked about their exit strategy –almost as though it's somehow disloyal to think about it. However, as author Steven Covey writes in *The 7 Habits of Highly Effective People* (Simon & Schuster, 1989): 'Always start with the end in mind.'

One very good reason for this is that it's worth bearing in mind that the decisions made on day one can have huge implications down the line. Having an exit strategy will make a lot of those decisions easier.

In this chapter we'll look at:

▶ why you shouldn't get too attached to a business

▶ where to get professional advice

▶ exit strategies.

You can't get too attached to a business

James Green has built and sold four tech companies. The lesson he learned is a hard one for most business owners: sometimes you can get too attached to a business.

'The one thing I wish I'd known when I started a business is that I shouldn't get emotionally attached to it,' Green says. 'Companies have no feelings, they are things, not people. Put bluntly, companies are here for one reason and one reason alone: to make money. Everyone knows that money can't buy you love, and by extension it makes no sense to love your company. There may come a time when you have to change it, dissolve it, close it, give it to someone else to run, cede control to investors, or any other number of things.' (**http://www.businessinsider.com/**)

Get professional advice

There are many different ways to value a business and plan for an exit. We strongly advise that you should seek advice from your accountant or a specialist as soon as possible in the process. Try to find someone who has a good track record of dealing with your type of business.

Seek advice from your accountant or a specialist as soon as possible.

If the business is going to carry on without you, the most important thing is to keep customers, staff, suppliers and any other stakeholders informed, reassured and happy. This will greatly enhance the value of the business to whoever takes it on.

Exit strategies

1   **Let it die with you.** A lot of negative things are said about so-called 'lifestyle' businesses, mostly because many of them don't make much money and are run specifically for the business owner to enjoy a good lifestyle. These business owners are sometimes accused of creating a job for themselves rather than a business, but if it is a job that gives the business owner the lifestyle they crave, what's wrong with that? These business owners will typically pay themselves, and often other family members, generous salaries rather than reinvesting money in growing the business. They are not really interested in what becomes of the business after they retire, but do need to plan for tax and pensions.

2   **Plan a succession.** An employee or family member can be groomed to take over as managing director or managing partner, and the business will have invested in pension plans to pay the retiring founder without affecting the revenue of the business. Succession planning can be a great way to make sure there is a smooth transfer from person to person and can be a great motivator for the person chosen as a successor. True planning is the key here, as the role and its skill requirements may change between when you decide upon a successor and when they are ready to move into the job.

3 **Sell to a friendly buyer.** Selling a business to a fan, loyal customer, employee, children or other family members can satisfy all sorts of emotional needs. Often in this kind of sale, the seller finances the sale and lets the buyer pay it off over time. This can sometimes lead to a business being sold for less than it would get by other means because of the emotional attachments.

4 **Acquisition**. This is one of the most common exit strategies: you find another business that wants to buy yours and sell it for a negotiated price. This is all about perceived value. The acquirer will put more value on your business if it allows them to expand into a new market, or offer a new product to their existing customers. Economic conditions also have a considerable impact when selling your business. For example, in a strong climate, your business should be able to capitalise by attracting a higher selling price. However, when economic conditions are less favourable your business may suffer in spite of your well applied talent, product ideas and overall best efforts. Be aware that buyers may be reluctant to pay the full price you feel you deserve, until they see the end of a downturn in economic conditions for the business.

5 **Going public (IPO)**. Most people who start a business with an exit strategy in mind will be dreaming of the day they can take the business public and sell shares in it. An Initial Public Offering or stock market launch gets a lot of attention because it means that total strangers think your business is worth investing in. However, it is a hugely expensive process and once your business is public, it is no longer your own. Very few small businesses ever get to this point.

Expert opinion Toni Hunter FCCA ACA DChA, George Hay, Chartered Accountants

Owners of SMEs struggle to get true worth from their business when they retire for one reason and one reason only.

They don't plan EARLY enough.

To truly give yourself the best chance you need a minimum of three years planning your exit.

▶

For example, the business may own a property that could be transferred to a pension scheme to provide a low-risk income stream, or there may be an element of the business that the owner really enjoys that could be separated off into a different business to provide a part time, lower key, more fun activity for semi-retirement.

I think there a few reasons why many SME owners don't think about planning for exit early enough. The key ones are:

▶ They're unaware of what is actually achievable if they have the right support and motivation.

▶ They have given up so much of their working lives creating the business they just can't see themselves leaving it, or can't envisage the business surviving without them.

▶ They are far too busy working *in* their business to take a good look further than a few weeks or months ahead.

One of the biggest barriers to selling a business is the impact of extracting the business owner. Owners are the glue that holds the whole enterprise together and without them, the business is just an arrangement of people and assets.

To get the best possible value, or in fact any offer at all, you need to be able to demonstrate that the business can generate a return on investment for the new owner without them needing to fill your shoes. This is actually simpler than it sounds, but it takes time.

The first step is to identify the most profitable areas of your business and focus on them, shedding the rest. Often small businesses are too diverse because they have morphed over time. Secondly, procedures and systems need to be smooth, efficient and above all tried and tested so that, within reason, your team members can take full responsibility for day-to-day operations. Finally, you need to ensure the market place knows who you are and what you do that is so fabulous. Brand value and customer retention is the key to recurring sales for the new owner.

It can take just minutes to create a procedure, hours to communicate it thoroughly, weeks for your team to properly learn it and months, perhaps even years for it to become the cultural norm. So get started NOW.

Good practice

We asked James Lawlor of Lawlor's Property Services about the experience of selling his family owned business while managing to keep it in the family:

> 'When we started we didn't have an exit strategy in mind as all my wife and I wanted to achieve was to run our own business as a lifestyle choice and to be independent and in control of our own destiny. I had been in a successful estate agency practice for over 11 years and felt unfulfilled. My wife had an eye on the broader picture to build a business and eventually sell but this was not our main goal.

> Our main goal was survival rather that exit strategies and that was the case for at least the first five years. Once the business had a track record of consistent profits over a period of three years we maybe should have looked at the value so we could at least have the option of selling if it made sense.

> We had considered selling when we had turned 50 but the recession hit in 2007/8 and took away that option. We reviewed our business model and made changes to the way we ran the business and our son, Elliott, had by that time proved that he had sufficient skills and commitment to the business to join our partnership. We then continued to develop and invest in the business with the view that my wife and I would continue to work but gradually pass more of the day-to-day running to Elliott as the face and the future of Lawlor's.

> We were approached by LSL PLC who recognised that our Lawlor's brand was a prestige acquisition for them as they wanted to take advantage of the emerging recovery in the residential market and exploit our prime position at the top end of the market. Their approach allowed us to accelerate some of our projects that were already in the pipeline.

> LSL had acquired many estate agencies so took into account our market position, our succession plan with Elliott at the helm and our past, present and projected profits. A figure was negotiated based on a multiple of the profits with a substantial proportion paid immediately and an earn-out

final payment based on sustaining and improving profits over the next three years.

The process felt exciting because of the many possibilities it opened up for Elliott as the youngest Managing Director in the LSLi Group and with the support of a PLC helping him grow the business far beyond the levels we could have hoped to achieve as a family. It also allowed my wife and me to accelerate our own personal and commercial plans and secure our future without compromising our son's.

We consulted with the whole family before making the final decision and it would have been easy to be sentimental and over-protective towards the business especially as it was an integral part of all of our lives for many years but the deal felt right for everyone so it was agreed. It was a fairly intrusive process but because my wife had run a very organised accounting system most of the required information was to hand to allow due diligence to be completed as efficiently as possible. However this was still a very complicated and exhausting process.

With hindsight we would probably have insisted on a small team of experts from LSLi to help us co-ordinate the due diligence process as often different departments required similar information and this caused more work than necessary.

Anyone who is thinking of an exit should understand that it is vital that the business should have systems in place that empower the management and staff to run it effectively without relying on the owners for every decision. If the business can't run without you then nobody will want to buy it.

We would also recommend selling a business before the top of the market is reached as the incoming purchaser will be more interested if they see growth in the business rather than a firm at its peak and maybe set for a decline.

Also consider the impact on the sale of the business on those that helped you achieve your profits as they may affect the future growth, especially if you need to still be involved with it after the sale.'

> Next steps
>
> ▶ Plan your exit – what strategy will you work towards?
> ▶ Consider how this will affect the decisions you need to take as you grow your business.

A closing note

Thank you for reading our book. If you have any questions about how to apply the information to your business or would like to keep up to date with the latest information, interviews and case studies, please join us at **www.newbusinessnextsteps.com**, we'd love to see you there.

What did you think of this book?

We're really keen to hear from you about this book, so that we can make our publishing even better.

Please log on to the following website and leave us your feedback.

It will only take a few minutes and your thoughts are invaluable to us.

www.pearsoned.co.uk/bookfeedback

Index